Get to the point

An anthology by Rugby Cafe Writers

Edited by John Howes and Theresa Le Flem

A CIP catalogue record of this book is available from the British Library.

ISBN-13: 979-8609227034
ASIN: B089D3FNSP

Contents

Acknowledgements

With grateful thanks to St. Andrew's Church, the Town Church, Rugby, for continuing to welcome and encourage local writers into the café. Also, thank you to all the wonderful staff and volunteers in the church's Thirteen Bells Café, for their friendly service and patience in hosting our fortnightly meetings, which can, at times, occupy more than its fair share of tables and chairs! Thank you all.

Cover design courtesy of Ealesh Patel.

Introduction

Running for over three years now, Café Writers is a lively gathering of local writers, poets and playwrights; we meet simply to talk about our work over a coffee. All of us have one thing in common: we need encouragement and advice, and we enjoy sharing our journey along that hazardous road into print. Our meetings run fortnightly on a Friday morning throughout the year without a break. We usually choose a topic to discuss, anything from tackling writer's block to how to promote sales of our books. An average of fourteen of us meet in the Thirteen Bells Café, inside St. Andrew's Church, in Rugby town centre.

A few years ago, during an author talk I gave for the Rugby Festival of Culture, I was surprised by the number of writers in the audience. Their questions led to a conversation continuing long after my allocated time, as people discovered their common interest – writing! This gave me the idea to start up the opportunity for these writers to meet again and get to know each other, and hence Café Writers was born.

Since that day, I'm proud to say some of them who were still finding their way then, are now published authors. More recently, several of us have taken Café Writers out to literary festivals in Southam and Northampton and given talks and book-signings locally. The curiosity the general public has in the mysterious world of a writer is, it seems, never dimmed; in fact, by sharing our experiences, we enjoy encouraging others not only to buy our books but to set out on that journey themselves. Some have always dreamt of doing this, but never taken the first step. The common saying that 'everyone has a book in them' is, we have discovered, surprisingly true.

So, we hope you enjoy reading this selection and trust it will inspire you to look further into our work, to purchase our books (links to which you will find at the back) and understand a writer's passion. Perhaps this might even prod you into putting pen to paper yourselves. There are always more stories out there, just waiting to be written. And if you live locally and would like to join us, there's always room for one more.

Theresa Le Flem

Foreword

A couple of years ago, I wandered into St Andrew's Church in Rugby and found the Cafe Writers gathering for one of their fortnightly meetings. Tea and coffee cups were clinking and there was a hubbub of friendly book-focused chat.

Ever since then, I have been a regular attender. To begin with, I felt a bit of a fraud. I hadn't written a book: I hadn't written a short story. I had a background in local newspaper journalism and, over a career spanning 25 years, had written hundreds of articles in print and online. But, as to fiction, I was a newcomer.

However, I had one big thing in common with everyone else around the table: I loved books. That is something of an understatement. I am obsessed with books as the many piles around my house will confirm. At any one time, I have perhaps ten or so books on the go. Sometimes it takes me ages to finish them, but that doesn't matter. It's the feel, the smell, the hidden delights awaiting in them.

And that was enough to make me feel at home with this inspirational group. There is an eclectic mix of people. Some are successful professional writers whose books have appeared in best-seller lists. Others have self-published novels whilst some are keen amateur poets. We all love writing and we love books.

Each time, we have a loose theme for our discussion - humour, anti-heroes, romance, opening lines, blurbs and so on. People bring along either something they have written themselves or an example of something they admire in the writing of others. We also exchange news on our own projects and, often, there is the wonderful moment of someone revealing their latest published book. There is always an ooh and an aah as the book is carefully passed around the group. What do we think of the cover? What does it smell like? Are we pleased with the typography and layout?

Several times a year, writers from the group take a table at various literary festivals to promote their books. We're not talking about hundreds of sales, but to sell a dozen might be a good day - even a couple can give you a good feeling.

In a time when reading could be seen to be on the decline, especially amongst young people, it is encouraging to see so many talented writers around, exploring so many different genres. Perhaps when you read this selection, you might think that you, too, have a book or a poem you would like to share. Perhaps you might want some advice on how to get it into print or online. You might just love books and want to talk about them.

If that is the case, please find out more by visiting our Rugby Cafe Writers Facebook group. In the meantime, we hope you enjoy this varied collection. There is something for everyone here from poetry to short stories to non-fiction. At the back of the book, you will find information about the authors with some links to their own websites.

John Howes

Bird

Paul Bird stood in front of the mirror and admired himself. He normally hated fancy dress. He didn't know why the marketing department always insisted that his company have a party every year, and then even worse have a stupid theme attached to it.

He hadn't noticed that costume shop before, although he must have passed it every day on the way home from work. That's how much he hated getting dressed up in silly outfits.

This bird costume was the one exception to his no fancy dress rule. As soon as he'd seen it, he'd been strangely drawn to it. It was quite spectacular, with sparkling red plumage and a satin sheen. How could he say no?

He pulled the top of the costume over his head like a hood and fiddled with it slightly to make sure the eye holes were in the right place to give him perfect vision. Then he took one last look at the bright costume, like he was modelling it on a catwalk.

It wasn't like a bird he'd ever seen. Red faux feathers were neatly complemented by the yellow and green streaks that covered his hands. He stroked the incredibly soft fabric. It felt so comfortable.

The doorbell rang and it was his cue to leave. He placed his feet in the clawed, yellow shoes, shoved his wallet in a little side compartment that he'd found, and he headed for the taxi.

*

The music was pumping as he arrived in the hall of his company's annual summer party. Bright lights bounced around the walls and the ceiling glistened against the reflection of the disco ball.

It seemed like such a waste of money to him, but he'd been nagged into it by his management team who swore it would be good for morale. The decent salaries he paid, that was good for morale. This was just being greedy.

He glanced around the room for anyone he would be willing to speak to. He hated making small talk with employees, especially when he had no clue who they were. And it was even more difficult on a night like tonight. All he could see was Little Bo-Peep by the bar, Dracula heading for the toilets and Bonnie and Clyde hitting the dancefloor early.

'Bird by name, bird by nature. You weren't kidding when you said it was quite a costume,' a man's voice said from behind him.

Paul turned around to be greeted by a white sheet. 'Hi Dave,' he said, acknowledging the Sales Director.

'How did you know it was me?' he laughed.

'No one else would be so cheap.'

'This is a masterpiece!' Dave argued.

'You haven't even cut the eye holes straight.'

'My wife did that. We were in a rush.'

'Figures. So you like my costume?'

'It's nice to see you make an effort for a change.'

'It's amazing isn't it? Here, feel the feathers.' Paul held out his arm for Dave to feel.

'It's not real feathers is it?'

'Don't be stupid. But they're so soft.'

Dave reluctantly flicked one of the wings, but he didn't react.

'Well?' Paul asked.

'Well what?' Dave took a gulp of his beer.

'It's incredible isn't it?'

'I suppose.' Dave just shrugged. Paul couldn't believe his lack of reaction. The costume felt like nothing he'd ever touched before. It was like silk to the fingers.

'Pint?' Dave asked, knocking the last of his drink back.

'If you insist,' Paul replied with a smirk.

*

It was midnight before Paul knew it and he was climbing into the back of his taxi home. It had been a really good night for a change, and he truly had been the spotlight in his impressive costume. Definitely a night to remember.

He got home, more inebriated than he'd planned on being, and staggered straight up the stairs in his detached house. Heading into his bedroom, he reached round to grab the zip at the back of his costume, but he couldn't find it. The soft plumage was quite thick, and it hadn't been easy to fasten, but he was sure there was a large piece of material to grab that would help manoeuvre the zip. He felt around again, twisting his arms back as far as he could.

He struggled for about ten minutes but there were just too many feathers in the way. Far more than he remembered there being.

Whether it was the effect of trying too hard or the effect of the alcohol, Paul suddenly started to feel quite dizzy. He lay on the bed, giving in. Meaning to try again in a few minutes, sleep beat him to it and his eyes slowly closed, sending him off into a deep, warm and comfortable sleep.

*

It was ten-thirty on Saturday morning when Paul naturally woke up. He rubbed his eyes and yawned, slowly bringing his hungover-self back to reality. He sat up and rested his feet on the carpet – or at least what he expected to be carpet. Instead his bare feet hit a soft, light material. He looked down and noticed a mass of red feathers cluttering the floor. It was his bird costume, destroyed all over his blue carpet.

Paul picked up a piece of the silky fabric and he was taken aback. Not like the night before, it now looked like real feathers. Shiny and red, just like the costume, but in every other way they were real looking feathers.

Paul swallowed. A sharp pain shot up his spine and he tried to make sense of what lay before him. He recalled not being able to find the zip, then that's all he could remember. Had he ripped it off in a state of panic?

Deciding he was far too hungover to deal with it, he threw his dressing gown on and headed to his kitchen. Despite it being the middle of July, he felt a cold chill wrap around him and he toyed with the idea of turning the heating on. Maybe he just needed coffee.

He filled his kettle and flicked it on and then made his way into the living room to take a seat. What was he going to do about that costume?

He stood up and headed to the mirror that resided over the fireplace. He wanted to take a look at himself. He was feeling a little alien in his own skin. Before he could take a proper look, though, he saw something behind him.

He turned around to see what was there, but there was nothing out of the ordinary. Composing himself, blaming too much drink, he turned to look at his reflection one more time. And this time he got a clear view. This time he saw, with no doubt, a man standing behind him.

He jumped around, ready to defend himself against the trespasser, but again there was no one there.

Terror burst through his soul as he recalled the face. He knew that man, but from where?

He looked back at the mirror, trying to work out why the face was so familiar, but all he could see this time was himself.

Keeping calm, he sat down. Then, like a flash, he remembered. He raced upstairs to grab his wallet. He pulled out a business card, one that he'd been given the day before at the fancy dress shop. That's who the man was: he was the owner of the shop.

Paul looked back to the floor where the scattered pile of feathers lay. He must be feeling more guilty than he thought. Deciding honesty was the best policy, he reached for his phone from the bedside table and dialled the number on the business card. He'd just pay whatever compensation was required and get it over with.

'Hello, Diamonds Jewellers,' a female voice answered.

'Who?' Paul asked.

'Diamonds Jewellers.'

'Sorry, I must have the wrong number. I was looking for Desruc fancy dress hire.'

'Sorry, never heard of it.'

'This is 842651?'

'Yes, that's our number.'

A sickening sensation lurched in his stomach. 'You're not at 21 Marking Street?'

'Yes. Can I help?'

'Do you know of any fancy dress shops?'

'There aren't any around here, I don't think.'

Paul hung up. His mouth dried and he couldn't breathe properly. What was going on?

Paul brought his fingers to his mouth to chew on his nails. A lifetime habit he'd never cared to change. But as his finger touched his lip, he stopped. It felt weird. He moved his hand down to look, and there, under every nail, were sprouts of red fluff.

*

Things hadn't improved by Monday morning. The feathers were still scattered all over Paul's bedroom carpet and he'd tried everything to remove the red fluff from his fingers, but it refused to go. It was as if it was now part of him.

He called in sick at work and deliberated over his options. Should he seek medical help? What had caused this? What had happened to that fancy dress shop? He sat on the sofa in his living room, trying to decide what to do, when he noticed he was scratching his arm. Pulling the sleeve of his sweatshirt up he looked in horror. There, in the middle of his arm, was a bright red feather.

*

The days passed by and the feathers multiplied. They were now sprouting up all over his body. He'd covered himself head to toe in clothes, like he was dressed for the middle of winter, just so he could get some supplies, and then he kept his front door firmly locked, too scared of what might happen to him next. He didn't know what to do.

His arms were now completely smothered in feathers and he was terrified. He wanted to scream, to shout for help, he wanted someone to make it all go away and comfort him. But he was all alone. He always pushed everyone away and now he finally did need someone he had no one to turn to.

*

Days turned into weeks and Paul grew more and more frightened. He'd told his work he had family commitments and wouldn't be around for a while. At least being the owner of the company, no one questioned it. He was so hungry, but his face was now covered in red fuzz and he was too afraid to leave the house. He'd ordered in, just throwing a well covered arm around the door to collect items, but that was now getting more difficult as with every passing day he noticed the world around him getting bigger; and that meant just one thing: he was shrinking.

*

A month had gone by since the party; since he'd worn that costume. Paul stood in front of the mirror in his bedroom and he felt a sense of déjà vu. In every way it looked like he was wearing that bird costume again, but it was now all completely attached to him. And he was half the size that he'd been before.

A tear rolled down the silky red feathers that surrounded his brown eyes, and past the yellow beak that was growing from his face. It was horrific and painful and he had never been so scared.

He didn't know what to do. He felt trapped in a horrid nightmare that was never going to end.

Every step was like walking on pins and his voice was barely audible. This was like a death sentence and he was riddled with regret. 'If only' scenarios fogged up his head but he was lost for ideas as to what he could do. He wanted the world to help him but he was too ashamed for anyone to see.

*

'Paul!' Dave shouted, banging on the front door of Paul's massive house. 'It's Dave, let me in.'

It had been weeks since anyone had heard from Paul and Dave knew it was time to take action. He'd first of all tried calling Paul's family, but they hadn't heard a thing either; not that they seemed very concerned about it. And now standing at Paul's front door, Dave could see that all three of Paul's cars were parked on his massive driveway. He had to be at home.

'Paul!'

Suddenly Dave heard what could only be described as a squawk from inside the house.

'Paul, are you all right?' Panic hit Dave. He knew he should have checked sooner. What if Paul was hurt? He owed it to Paul to check.

The squawk got louder.

Dave banged again on the door, but he knew it was pointless. No one was coming. Something was wrong. He stepped back in an attempt to knock the front door down, but it wouldn't budge. It was a seriously strong door. Instead, Dave moved around to the windows. He glared in but he couldn't see anything.

Then something caught his eye; something moved. Suddenly, flying, as if to greet him, then sitting on the window ledge inside the house, Dave saw a little red bird.

It squawked at him as if it was trying to communicate.

'Do you know where Paul is?' Dave asked the bird, before he rolled his eyes. What was he doing talking to a bird?

He looked again closer at it. He studied it, through the glass of the window, and he saw a tear appear in the corner of the bird's eye. The droplet then fell to the ledge. The bird was crying. This beautiful red bird in front of him was crying.

Lindsay Woodward

The Shoes

The shoes stood in the centre of the shop window. They were so lovely, thin strips of gold leather with tall, slender heels decorated with crystals. They would look amazing with my black evening gown, the Shirley Bassey one with sparkly spaghetti straps and the split to the top of my thigh. The perfect shoes for the perfect outfit!

I already had a gold evening bag and a wrap of shimmering shot silk. I was going to look absolutely fabulous.

The shop was one of those small exclusive boutiques where there are no prices in the window. The shoes would be very expensive as they were designer, but worth every penny. I opened the door and the bell chimed elegantly. Inside, the shoes and boots were arranged on the shelves like pieces of art, only one pair of each style on display. In the middle of the shop, the handbags reclined on a long oak table that had been polished until it shone like a mirror.

The saleswoman stared at me as I picked up one of the gold evening sandals. She wore a well-cut black suit and her make-up was immaculate. Her hair looked as if it didn't move.

'Can I help you?' she said, not meaning a word of it.

'Do you have these in an eight?' I asked.

'I'll have to check,' she said, not moving. 'We don't sell many eights. It's rather a large size.'

I didn't answer. Eventually she moved herself to the storeroom. In spite of her smart appearance, she was wearing decidedly un-chic flat brown lace-ups. It must be very hard on her feet, all that running about and attending to customers.

I looked at the other shoes. There was a beautiful pair of white peep-toe courts with butterflies on the toes, just right for a summer wedding. Next to them was a pair of olive-green suede boots with pink stitching on the seams. I loved them too, but I had plenty of boots, even if none of them was green. On the shelf below was a pair of metallic pink mules with kitten heels. There was a matching bag and I was so tempted, but I had to be strict with myself. I was here for the gold evening sandals.

The saleswoman returned and handed me the box. 'Here you are,' she said ungraciously. I opened the box. The shoes nestled together, wrapped in tissue. I took them out. They were so beautiful.

'I'd like to try them on.' I took off my trainers and socks.

A strangled noise came from the saleswoman, but my feet are always well cared for and the crimson nail polish was immaculate. I rolled up my jeans and slipped the shoes on, carefully fastening the straps, then stood up. They were a perfect fit. The saleswoman's eyes were bulging. I walked up and down, turning in front of the mirror. Fabulous.

'I'll take them.' I took off the shoes and handed them to her. She took the shoes and the box to the till while I put my socks and trainers back on. I walked over to her and presented my credit card. She snatched it out of my hand and shoved it in the machine. I entered my PIN. Transaction completed; she gave me the bag with my new shoes inside.

I've always had small feet for a man.

Fran Neatherway

Quick Poem

(R.I.P. D.M.C.)

Here we go
bom bom bom
Hah
Poets!
get to the point
get to the point
get to the point and
Quickly!!
quick quick quick quickly

I had to write some verse
in time it turned out worse
gave it some thought
it came to naught
and now I start to curse

My warehouse work is boring
and mostly worth ignoring
pointless meeting
bust-up heating
Boss is out and snoring
Novelists,
get to the point
get to the point
get to the point and
Quickly!!
quick quick quick quickly

Playwrights,
get to the point
get to the point
get to the point and
Quickly!!
quick quick quick quickly

My words as sweet as Honey
My rhymes are often Funny
I hate to speak it
Time to leak it
I want to earn cheap money

Let's start a revolution
A national solution
So write it fast
It may not last
It's literary pollution

Authors,
get to the point
get to the point
get to the point and
Quickly!!
quick quick quick quickly

Speakers,
get to the point
get to the point
get to the point and
Quickly!!
quick quick quick quickly

Chairmen,
get to the point
get to the point
get to the point and
Quickly!!
quick quick quick quickly

DONE
(folds arms)

Chris Wright

My Grandmother's Watch

My grandmother's wrist was small as a child's
but she was forceful, proud,
I weighed the faded gold half-hunter watch in my palm
wound it, shook it, put it to my ear
Still nothing
not a single heartbeat's tick
I can hear her now complaining, about this, that,
and 'this lousy government'
'can't wait to get back to the Island'
she said, and she did

The chain link wristband clinked,
the smooth worn gold warmed in my hand
I smelt again her fur coat, sleek as a fox
her handkerchief, her Eau de Cologne
her sugar-coated almonds

I willed her watch to work, stared at its tiny pale face
It looked back at me
over shared years, wartime,
young married life, children, children's children,
rations, each tick had a price, each morsel savoured
precious, nothing wasted

She would have made sure her watch kept pace,
my grandmother's tongue would have clicked
with impatience, she had no time
for things that wouldn't work

I took it to be repaired
'Hello, Harry' I said,
above the rattle of a thousand clocks,
'Can you do something with this?'
A magnifying glass appeared
the warmed gold was laid bare on his leather desk
all its history undone,
'Yes,' he said, 'give me time.'

Theresa Le Flem

Dancing with Daddy

Little Pink Boots grips Daddy's arm
with both hands, leans back and
with all her weight, pulls Daddy
to his feet and onto the stone slabs
of the abbey square. Daddy's long legs
tower over Little Pink Boots. She holds
Daddy's hands and twists and turns
her little pink boots hopping and skipping
her long frock dipping and swirling to the beat.

Daddy's feet are planted on the ground
his back bent at a right-angle. He twirls her
under and round, under and round
and swings her up in a great carousel
higher than his kind eyes, higher than
his gentle smile. Her skirts flare out
her dark hair streaming. Her little pink boots
peep from her frills as she orbits him
like a planet worshipping the sun.

All the ladies sitting round the square
want to fly like Little Pink Boots. Oh,
how they wish they were Little Pink Boots
dancing with Daddy in the square!

Wendy Goulstone

Driven

Darren had just given the finger to the driver of a Honda Jazz. The elderly lady looked terrified. Although Darren had been in the wrong - trying to barge out of a parking space without looking - there was no way he was going to admit it. He felt superior in his black Subaru and, as far as he was concerned, he was the perfect driver. He had customised his vehicle - the vented hood, the large spoiler, the purple avant garde wheels.

Fast reflexes were a godsend to Darren and he was prepared to take risks to reach his destination quickly. The salesman had promised the motor was powerful enough to 'get you out of trouble'. And Darren had plenty of opportunity to put this to the test. He was an important man and couldn't waste time in unnecessary traffic queues or behind slow drivers.

As he flattened his foot on the accelerator, Darren felt good, snaking away through the retail park and out onto the dual carriageway. Reaching the lights, he wound down the window and ejected a still-lit cigarette butt. A flick on his windscreen cleaner sent a jet of water over the roof of his vehicle and onto the car behind. Darren checked his mirror. The other driver was irritated. Good.

Darren's driving was on the edge of the law. He liked to push the limits. He always drove with his headlights and fog lights on: it made him feel like a rally driver. He always had Radio 1 booming out of his sound system. He was getting a bit old for it and secretly preferred Radio 2. But that didn't fit his image: cool, fast, a magnet for the ladies. Or so he reckoned.

Today, Darren was not going to work. He'd taken the morning off. The IT helpdesk could run itself for a while. It wasn't by choice. He'd been 'invited' to a safe driving course after being caught doing 39mph in a 30mph zone. But he didn't tell anyone he was doing the course, located at a nearby hotel on the ring road.

Imagine his anger - and Darren had big anger issues - when he turned up two minutes late. The traffic was terrible, he lied, when really it was Treacy's fault for failing to wake him in time.

Sorry, sir. We can't admit you, said the jobsworth clerk holding a clipboard.

Two minutes! Who cares about two minutes? argued Darren. He was starting to get annoyed. He wasn't the calmest of people at the best of times - and when it was anything to do with driving, he was like a coiled spring.

To cut a long argument short, Darren was not admitted to the course, which would have avoided costly points on his licence. The jobsworth explained the reason and suggested he contact the office again. There might be another course in a couple of months.

But I've taken the morning off work. This has cost me, affirmed the increasingly irritated Darren. He screwed up his coffee cup and threw it in the direction of the bin - but missed.

Tossers, he muttered in a voice just loud enough to be heard, as he turned for the exit, slamming the door behind him.

Darren was about to fire up his engines when another vehicle slid into the parking space next to him, on his left. It was a small, grubby, inferior car driven by a middle-aged man with greying hair. The man turned his engine off and opened his door. Thwack! The door hit Darren's passenger door. Actually, the sound was nearer to Fttt, because it wasn't a big connection - hardly anything in fact. But it was enough to get Darren roused into a molten fury. He flung open his door and confronted Mr Grey Hair.

Was that my car you hit? (Darren)

I'm terribly sorry. I was miles away. It was only a light tap. (Mr Grey Hair)

You hit my car. What do you think you're doing? You're going to pay for this. (Darren)

Darren edged closer to Mr Grey Hair until his forehead was nearly touching him.

Let's have a look at the door. (Mr Grey Hair).

Together, they looked at Darren's passenger door. There wasn't a mark on it.

There doesn't seem to be any damage. I really am sorry. I should've taken more care. (Mr Grey Hair).

Darren turned away in disgust. There was nothing that appalled him more than someone else being in the right.

Arsehole. (Darren)

Back behind the wheel, and master of the road, Darren turned for home. His car had a device fitted which automatically slowed him down when he got too close to the driver in front. Darren loved this feature because it meant he could drive to within a few centimetres of irritating slow motorists who insisted on keeping within the speed limit. It allowed him to join their slipstream and creep right up to their bumpers, headlights flashing to get them to move out of the way or speed up.

This was especially useful on dual carriageways and motorways. Darren owned the outside lane and no one was going to impede his progress. And if a driver

GET TO THE POINT

unreasonably declined to move out of the way, then he would cut to the inside lane, or even the hard shoulder, to undertake him.

The route home took Darren along a very straight piece of road heading towards the horizon and over a lowish hill. He loved this way because he could floor his foot and watch the Subaru's speed leap towards three figures. It also made him think of the States, those long highways heading into the distance: a land where the driver ruled the road, no namby-pambies talked about green fuel and all that climate warming crap.

Good. There were no other drivers around. Darren's foot pressed down and the engine gunned into action. This wasn't a driver's seat: it was a cockpit. And Darren was about to zoom into the skies.

Ahead of him, a couple of crows were making a meal out of some roadkill. Bash. Darren sent one flying whilst the other made a last-second getaway.

Suddenly, on the horizon, Darren spotted a vehicle heading in his direction. It was certainly shifting. Well, two could play at that game.

Darren pushed down a bit harder on the accelerator. He adjusted his baseball cap to block out the glint of the sun. He was going to enjoy this.

The other car must have been doing 80mph, maybe 90mph. It was black and, as it came closer, he noticed it was a Subaru, just like his.

Strange coincidence. There weren't that many around. And yes, it had the vented hood and the spoiler. And, hold on, weren't those purple wheels like his? Interesting. Well he wasn't going to be intimidated by it.

Now, the cars were maybe half a mile apart and Darren could just about make out the driver. A man, about his age, and he was wearing a baseball cap.

This is weird, thought Darren. He's driving the same car as me and he looks like me.

Then, and only then, Darren got a good look at the man's face. Close-cut beard, beady eyes, thin-looking and a bit aggressive. It was Darren to a tee. It was Darren's face. It was like he was looking in a mirror. He had met his own double driving his own car. And it was heading towards him at speed.

Should he just drive by and, maybe, give the finger to this imposter? Should he feint a swerve to push this dickhead off the road? How dare someone try to be Darren? To out-Darren Darren, king of the road.

They were a couple of hundred yards apart and, despite the speed, things seemed to happen in slow motion. Darren made the slightest of turns to the wheel as if he was going to drive into the path of the oncoming Subaru. The imposter did the same, at exactly the same time. Now they were both in the middle of the road and there was no going back. Darren realised that if the other driver had the same approach to driving as him, he was not going to back down either. They were both committed - and there could be only one result.

*

The police report soon went viral, mainly because it was so unbelievable. The twisted, melted remains of a Black Subaru were discovered on a long, straight, lonely road after a devastating head-on collision. Inside, firefighters discovered a charred body. Accident experts estimated the car had been driving in excess of 100mph when the collision occurred.

But strangest of all, and what got everyone talking, was that there was no second vehicle. Despite the ferocity of the crash, the other car was never found. No one reported to hospital with injuries and no vehicle ever turned up.

*

Somewhere, a bird sweetly sang. An autumn breeze blew gently. All was well.

John Howes

It's a Family Affair

Adam took the drinks and returned to the over-decorated table. 'Guess who's working the bar?' he said, handing Mona her wine.

Mona leaned back to catch a look at the barman. 'Hiya Pete!' She waved, and the lean-looking Australian waved back. She turned her attention back to Adam. 'Trust you to come to a wedding and know the barman,' she said, giving his arm a playful punch. Adam let out a long breath before taking a slug of his pint: it wasn't knowing the barman that was the problem.

As soon as he'd realised, he should have left but something had stopped him, something he didn't want to think too hard about. He was grateful that they weren't seated too close to the top table and that the ridiculous floral centrepiece was providing much needed cover for him to hide behind.

Mona hugged his arm through the Father of the Bride speech and wiped away a tear at the same time as the bride's father. When the groom got to his feet, Mona let out an uncharacteristic whistle, making Adam duck down behind the flowers.

'Sorry,' she said, 'but my little brother is really nervous.' The room fell silent and all eyes were on the groom apart from Adam's. Through the edge of the centrepiece foliage and dyed pink ostrich feathers, he stared at the bride. She looked more beautiful than he remembered and he had some amazing memories tucked away. Memories that he had spent two years pushing into the darkest recesses of his mind in an effort to move on. The groom choked on his words and the whole room let out an 'ahhhh' apart from Mona who shouted encouragement, 'Love you, Garth!'

'It's OK, that's my sister, not some old girlfriend!' said Garth with a nervous chuckle and the devoted audience laughed along with him, all except for the bride. Kirsty's face was suddenly a shade paler than her extravagant designer dress and she was staring at the hunched figure next to Mona who was trying to hide behind the cascading floral design. Garth stopped speaking and everyone stood up for the toast, blocking her view. Kirsty looked away and forced a smile onto her face. Her mother leaned forward.

'Are you all right, sweetheart?'

Kirsty nodded. 'Just a little overcome.'

'Ahh, how sweet. You two are just the cutest,' said Shelley, before repeating it to the groom's father.

'I can't believe you've got a daughter of Kirsten's age.' He absentmindedly smoothed his hand over his bald patch.

'I was a child bride,' whispered Shelley. 'They said it wouldn't last but we are still together and never happier.'

'I bet we'll be grandparents soon. You mark my words,' he said, as Shelley looked as if someone had just slapped her in the face with one of the organza-covered chairs.

'I'm only forty-three, I can't be a granny. I'm too young!' The words seemed to hang in the air and she took a long drink of champagne.

*

Adam had escaped as far as the bar. He knew he should leave but something was stopping him. He glanced over his shoulder: there was a clean escape route. He could just turn around and walk out but Mona would most likely never forgive him if he did. Sweet Mona: they had been getting close. Adam shook his head. He knew, if he wasn't very careful, today would change everything.

'What are you shaking your head for Ad?' came the barman's familiar accent.

'Pete, mate. I wouldn't know where to start.'

'Try me,' said Pete, scooting around the end of the bar to join Adam. There was nobody else there as everyone was listening to the Best Man droning on about the Groom's university years.

Adam shook his head but he caught the look in Pete's eye. He downed the rest of his pint and put down the glass. 'Do you remember me telling you about me and a couple of the guys from the Rugby club earning extra cash as topless waiters a few years back?'

'Remember? I've seen the photos! Like a cheap version of the Chippendales you were. All sorts of gorgeous females in your arms and a beautiful brunette eating strawberries off your six pack. That is the sort of gig I would love.'

Adam waved it away. 'It wasn't that great really.'

'Seriously? Those women were all over you. Hey, didn't you tell me you even hooked up with a birthday girl once?' Pete winked.

'Yep, that's the problem. She's here.'

*

Mona fidgeted in her seat. The Best Man was rambling now and he looked like he still had a couple of pages to read. She looked around again, this time trying to make it look like she was admiring the elaborately decorated room. She didn't want to look desperate but Adam had been gone a long while. He'd said he was going to the loo but she was now starting to wonder if he'd left. She chewed her lip. Maybe she was overthinking things. She needed to have more confidence. Why would he leave? They were getting on so well: the last four months had been the happiest she could remember.

Going out with her personal trainer was a bit of a cliché but what had started out as a confidence boost was definitely developing into something much stronger. He was totally gorgeous with a body to die for, he was thoughtful, articulate and loved animals – there was nothing not to like about him. Her old insecurities had tried to creep back in but she was managing to keep them at bay. Her only worry was whether Adam was feeling the same.

*

The Best Man handed out the gifts to the bridesmaids and everyone stood for the final toast. Adam snuck back into the room and made his way through the maze of raised arms and clapping hands.

'The bride and groom!' he chorused. As he reached Mona's side, she visibly relaxed and a smile played on her lips. She was really very pretty. Her dark hair hung in natural curls, her pale blue eyes were full of love for him. She was kind and funny and he'd felt more settled over the last few weeks with her than he had in the last two years. There was also something about her that made Adam want to protect her. He'd only ever felt like that once before.

'Are you OK?' asked Mona, when the clapping had stopped and people started to mill about unsure as to what was happening next.

'Actually, no. I've got the most awful headache. I was thinking about heading off. Would you be okay if I went?' Adam pleaded with his eyes.

'You poor thing. I've got painkillers. Here take these,' she said after rooting around in her clutch bag. 'Can I just introduce you to a few more relatives then we can both escape?'

It was more reasonable than Adam deserved. This was her brother's wedding and he was encouraging her to leave early for a fake headache: he could hardly explain the real reason was that he didn't want to be recognised. The longer they stayed, the more likely that became.

'Thanks, that would be great.' He gave a wince to emphasise his discomfort and swallowed the tablets. Mona took him by the hand and headed for the top table. Adam felt his stomach lurch and he desperately looked around for a distraction or something to conceal him. The cake was actually big enough but unfortunately not close enough for him to hide behind.

The top table had scattered but Mona was able to introduce him to the bridesmaids who were both chatty and quite upbeat despite the very large pink dresses they'd been forced to wear. The room was starting to empty out and the hotel staff were already rearranging the tables ready for the evening reception.

A very familiar voice with a questioning tone cut through the melee, 'Mona?'

Mona and Adam pirouetted around together and Kirsty looked from one to the other. Mona dropped Adam's hand and flung her arms around the bride. 'Kirsten, you're officially my sister-in-law!' she said excitedly, followed by a noise that sounded a lot like 'squeeeee'. She let her go and stood back as if to reveal Adam. He thought for a moment she was going to say 'Ta Dah!' 'And this is Adam. He's the little secret I told you I was keeping.'

They all stared at each other for a moment. Mona was practically glowing with pride. Adam recovered first and stepped forward to air-kiss the bride. 'Lovely to meet you Kirsten. It's been wonderful but Mona and I need to make a move,' he said, taking Mona's hand. Kirsty's gaze drifted down to their entwined fingers.

'We're not rushing off just yet,' cut in Mona, 'I need to show you off to a few more people first. It's a rare occasion that you get all your relatives in one place. Weddings and funerals and, if it's the latter, then someone is usually missing,' she said with a giggle.

Kirsty still said nothing. She was looking at Mona and Adam's hands as if something had made her brain freeze. Garth appeared behind her, grabbing her affectionately around the waist, which had a similar effect to defibrillation paddles and she almost gasped into life.

'I thought you'd left me already!' Garth nuzzled at Kirsty's neck. It was Adam's turn to feel like he'd been put on freeze frame. An icy sensation flooded his gut. Garth pulled away from his bride. 'Hiya, Sis. I've hardly seen you today,' he said to Mona.

Kirsty glanced at Adam and he blinked hard. This was his worst nightmare and he was wide awake and living it. 'Garth. This is Adam. Adam is Mona's boyfriend,' said Kirsty, the words sounding stilted as if she was reading from an autocue. The lighting dimmed and the music started.

'I know,' said Garth with a shrug. 'I met him weeks ago but Mona swore me to secrecy.' He gave Mona a nudge and shook hands with Adam. 'Come on, the DJ is setting up and we need to be ready for the first dance, then I have a little surprise for you.' He gave her a kiss and Adam felt his heart ache at the sight. 'Right, we'll catch you two lovebirds later,' said Garth, as he towed Kirsty away.

Adam and Mona stood at the edge of the dance floor and watched the newlywed couple dance to their song. The other guests had now migrated back into the transformed room. As the bridesmaid and Best Man, Bride's Mother and Groom's Father paired off to dance, Adam had a moment of clarity. He squeezed Mona's hand and pulled her to him.

'You should dance with your brother.'

'Should I?' Mona seemed unsure. Adam gave what he hoped was a reassuring smile. Mona eased onto her tiptoes and kissed him. She skirted around some guests and, as the record changed, she stepped onto the dance floor.

'Can I have this dance?' she asked her brother.

Garth grinned at his sister. 'Sure. You don't mind do you, darling?' Kirsty shook her head. 'Don't go anywhere though,' he said firmly.

'May I?' said Adam as he took Kirsty's hand and felt her jolt at the contact. He pulled her to him and they danced away from Mona and Garth.

'What the hell are you doing here?' asked Kirsty, her voice a low threatening rumble.

'Mona said her brother was marrying someone called Kirsten. That was all I knew. I had no idea it was you, Kirsty.'

'Don't call me that,' she said before swallowing hard. 'I've left that person behind.' She tried to pull away but he kept hold of her and he felt her surrender.

'We need to talk,' he whispered.

'No, we don't. You left me and went to Dubai.' Emotion bubbled in her voice.

'You said you didn't want to see my shitty face ever again.'

'Because I was angry with you not because...' said Kirsty, her voice catching in her throat. Adam stopped dancing and stared at her. 'Kirsty you are such a beautiful person, and not just in looks. There's not a day gone by that...'

'Don't,' she whispered, breaking eye contact.

Kirsty's mother and father sashayed past them doing something similar to a waltz and Shelley did a double take at her daughter's dancing partner. Kirsty stepped in front of Adam to block her mother's view.

Mona and Garth were following them, doing a lap of the dance floor as they had gone all *Strictly Come Dancing* and they both grinned as they went by. Mona looked so happy. Adam felt like he was being pulled in two different directions by a force he couldn't control.

Adam and Kirsty were no longer dancing. 'I thought you hated me,' said Adam.

Kirsty half smiled. 'No, I could never hate you, Adam. Well, not for long.'

'So why did it change everything? The thing that happened...it was before we got together. I would never have hurt you.'

Kirsty's expression changed, her eyes filled with pain. The music started to fade but they were now barely aware of anyone else. Garth was taking the microphone from the DJ.

'But when I found out, it did hurt me,' said Kirsty, her voice getting louder as the music died.

'I'm sorry, but it was just a one-night thing at a

birthday party.'

'Not quite Adam! You slept with my mum at her fortieth!'

There was a small gasp from Shelley, followed by a thud.

Bella Osborne

Wave

There's a wave with my name on it, way out to sea
It's rolling this way, Westwards, coming to me
The water gathers, makes the grey-green wall rise
Stand in slack water, watch White Horses ride

Back to the horizon, lean forward and launch
Ride the waves inwards, pushed by their force
Straight as a board, feel the lift, feel the surge
The galloping of White Horses' hooves in your ears

E. E. Blythe

Cleopatra and Antony

'My own Cleopatra, Queen of the Nile
Come hither now and set this old heart free.
With your enticing smile, your wayward wiles,
your lusty infinite variety.'

Bathing in milk to preserve her beauty
painted Eunuchs fan her to keep her cool.
Handmaidens dance attendance to duty
While the Emperor Caesar looks the fool.

Mistress in turn, to two-thirds of the world
Power and sovereignty in her hand
Her plan to marry Antony now unfurled
She will reign supreme over all the land

Held lovingly in Lord Antony's arms
Cleopatra applied her seductive charms.

Madalyn Morgan

Spring as I see it

Green fields, hedged in by sprouting Hawthorn
Its leaves nearly fully unfurled.
Lime trees of lush mouth-watering hue,
The Sycamores are fully in leaf.
The Oak leaves have come out first this year
But the Ash buds are still as black as night.
Everywhere grows vigorously with each passing day.
There's dew in the morning
and darkness does not descend until gone nine o'clock.

Along our lanes the verges are succulent,
our spring flowers are scattered everywhere.
The magic Arum Lilies called Lords and Ladies
or Cuckoo Pint with broad purple blotched leaves.
There are still a few violets under the banks and pink
Campions can be seen now.
The white blossomed Black Thorn is magnificent
in its almost Bridal Glory.

Our Spring birds are with us.
The Blithe Cuckoo is almost a common sound
to our ears, cucking softly,
drowsily through the day until dusk has fallen.
The handsome Cock-pheasant gives his rasping,
warning cry as he takes to the air.

The Yellow-hammer in his greeny yellow plumage
The Chaffinch chink chinks incessantly
But it is the Blackbird's sweet voice that is my
inspiration

43

Those true golden notes as the evening progresses,
stirring my heart,
bringing a yearning within me and tears to my eyes.

Ruth Hughes

The Red Silk Dressing Gown

Her perfume lingered in the air, and the red silk dressing gown that she loved so much lay across the chair. I touched the teapot as I passed. It was still warm. She had left the small table lamp on. Its welcoming light spilt warmly onto the old rosewood dressing table. We used to have tea at that table - hot buttered toast and scones with jam. I can see her now, picking the strawberries from the jam when she thought I wasn't looking, then licking the sweet preserve from her fingers. She thought I wouldn't know. I always knew. Small sticky fingerprints on the polished surface were a giveaway. I traced, with my finger, where her tiny hands had been. The table was smooth to the touch, and as elegant today as it had been thirty years ago.

Was it really thirty years since I sat in front of that dressing table mirror and transformed myself into Cleopatra?

'This is your five-minute call, Miss Lester. Five minutes until curtain-up!' The stage manager poked his head around the dressing room door and winked at Alexandra. 'Nanny's waiting for you at the stage door, Alexandra. If you're ready, I'll take you down.'

Standing on tiptoe, Alexandra had put her arms around my waist. 'You look beautiful, Mummy. When I grow up,' she said, taking a step back and looking up at me with big brown eyes, 'I shall be an actress, like you. Will you come and watch me play Cleopatra?'

'Of course, I will, darling.'

'Promise?'

'I promise.' I knelt down and kissed my daughter

goodbye. 'Nothing in the world would stop me.' And nothing did stop me. Although I hadn't reckoned on not being in the world when the time came.

Without warning, tears fell from my eyes. They were tears of pride and love - and perhaps of sadness too, because I was no longer part of my daughter's life. But, I had kept the promise I made to her when she was a child. Tonight, I had seen her play Cleopatra - and in a more truthful, more compelling way, than I had ever seen Cleopatra played before.

I watched her as she took her curtain-call, and I saw happiness and humility in her eyes as two thousand people stood up and applauded her. Presented with a bouquet, she turned and looked in my direction. As if she knew I was standing in the wings, she held the bouquet high in the air with one hand, blew a kiss with the other, and said, 'For you, Mum.'

It was then that I knew my daughter would always remember me, always love me, but she no longer needed me to watch over her.

Suddenly, laughter, the popping of champagne corks, and the indistinguishable chatter of people congratulating each other burst into the dressing room over the tannoy, bringing me back to reality. The first-night party had begun. That was my cue to leave.

I lifted the red silk dressing gown, which had once been mine, and held it against my cheek. Alexandra loved that old dressing gown. I had given it to her as a first-night present many years before when she made her stage debut. The sash was frayed, the silk was so worn it was almost transparent, but she took it everywhere. It was soft and smooth to the touch. It slipped through my fingers, falling gently onto the seat of the chair, the companion to the polished table.

I looked around the room for what I knew would be the last time. I wanted to savour the sweet smell of her perfume, the sound of applause and the laughter I could hear from the party. I closed my eyes and stood very still to soak up the atmosphere.

'This is your final call, Miss Lester.'

'What?'

'I'm sorry. I didn't mean to startle you, but our time is up,' the stage manager said.

'Our time?' I questioned.

'Yes. I also watched our daughter tonight.'

'Our daughter? How long have you known Alexandra was your child?'

'Not until I saw her on stage tonight. Watching her was like watching you thirty years ago.'

'I am so sorry I didn't tell you. Can you ever forgive me?'

He took my arm. 'It doesn't matter now,' he said, guiding me towards a door that I hadn't noticed before. I touched the teapot. It was cold. Before I reached the point of no return, I looked back. The lamp still shone its pale light across the polished table, and the red silk dressing gown still lay across the chair.

Madalyn Morgan

The Boy

Easing himself out of his cab, taxi-driver Fergus stood up, stretched and took a few deep breaths of the early morning air. He emptied his pipe by knocking it on the bumper several times before surveying the scene contentedly.

Being a self-employed taxi driver, the night shift was the time to earn the most cash, but it was an exhausting schedule. This was a typical autumn morning in London, full of anticipation as people hurried past on their way to work. For Fergus, it was the end of his shift and he was going to pick up his usual bacon buttie before heading out across the square to where his lodgings were, to sleep. Fergus had no home or family comforts to return to, but it didn't worry him. Married life was a distant memory, and, with his mother living in sheltered accommodation, his brother in the army and his father...

Well, his father could be anywhere; he hadn't had contact with him for years. Fergus found some change in his trouser pocket, and, leaving his cab parked, he wandered over to the news-stand, bought a newspaper and then joined the queue for hot dogs, bacon butties and doughnuts. In no time at all, armed with his breakfast and newspaper, Fergus walked back to his cab.

It was when he opened the cab door and climbed in that he noticed a child hiding in the back. A boy was sitting hunched up on the floor of the cab behind the driver's seat. Fergus acted as if he hadn't spotted him and sat in his cab comfortably, leaving the door ajar as was his custom unless wind and rain prevented it. He sank his teeth into the hot salty bacon buttie and spread his newspaper on his knees. This demonstration of total relaxation presumably confirmed in the boy's mind that his presence, for the moment, remained undiscovered. It also gave Fergus valuable thinking time.

He was trying to recall his last fare: did they have a child with them? He was so tired, and all his fares were a blur. As far as he could remember, they hadn't. Fergus had been driving people around all night and, after a while, it became so routine, he could hardly distinguish one journey from another. Backwards and forwards through London, picking up fares, dropping them off - they all became a sea of faces in the end. Being a Friday night, it had been busy, and he had had more than one disruptive, or drunk, passenger. But the money in his leather pouch was bulging and heavy.

He often worried about being robbed, which is why he kept the pouch strapped to his belt under his shirt. It was a bit uncomfortable, but at least he knew it was there. His mother had given him that pouch; it was made of nice soft leather – she had sewn it herself and given it to him for Christmas years ago. The cash would go back with him to his lodgings. He didn't trust deposit boxes. In fact, he didn't use a bank account at all: he kept all his takings back in his room in a special tin he kept in the fridge. Almost all that he saved went straight to his old mother. If he couldn't get to see her at weekends, he bundled it up in a load of polythene bags, wrapped it in a brown paper parcel and posted it off to her. She relied on the extra money he gave her: she could hardly get by on her pension alone, not in London. She wasn't an educated lady, but she was clever with her hands, knitted him warm jumpers and cooked him steak pies to take back to his lodgings.

Unknown to the boy, Fergus could glimpse the top of his head in the driver's rear-view mirror. He wondered how he had got there, but somehow he didn't feel able to actually ask him, or even to let him know that he had been discovered. So Fergus carried on eating and reading his newspaper, while he pondered on what to do. Finally, finishing the bacon buttie, he screwed up the bag and chucked it over his shoulder in a casual fashion, clearing his throat as he did so. It landed softly on the back seat. In his rear-view mirror, Fergus saw the boy jump up. The secret was out.

Turning and meeting the boy's eyes, he looked at him - a long sad look, as if the boy's whole history was written there on that haunted little face. Nodding, as if he understood something of the boy's distress, Fergus reached into his waistcoat, took out his pipe and began to fill it with tobacco, pressing it into the bowl of the pipe with his thumb. This was all part of his morning ritual. He moved so he was sitting half-inside, half-outside the driver's seat, struck a match and lit up.

'You smoke?' he asked finally. The boy shook his head. 'Good lad,' he replied. 'Glad somebody's sensible.' The words were offered in a cloud of fragrant tobacco smoke which was snatched up through the open door of the cab, up into the heights of London's plane trees and tall concrete buildings.

The boy rose out of his crouched position in the well of the car and perched nervously on the edge of the back seat. He was only about eight years old. Fergus saw the school blazer, the dirty white shirt, school tie askew; he looked as if he was once smartly dressed, and not that long ago.

'Not going to school today, are you? I mean, it's

Saturday you know!' said Fergus. The boy again shook his head. As yet, he hadn't spoken a word. 'What's your name, lad?' Fergus asked, speaking directly to him now; he needed to know. The boy turned his face away and gazed out of the window. But then, just as Fergus had given up on receiving an answer, his small husky voice came back.

'Gilbert, sir.'

'Gilbert! Is that your first name or your second name?' he asked. But the boy didn't reply so Fergus just repeated the name to himself, as if by saying it again it would give him a clue.

'Gilbert… mmm… Gilbert…' he mused, puffing on his pipe.

'Did I happen to take you and your mother or father somewhere this morning from St Pancras station?' he asked hopefully. That, he remembered, had been his last fare. 'It's my age, you know,' he added. 'My memory's not what it was.'

Again, there was, however, no reply. He tried again:

'Are you lost, Gilbert?' he asked, becoming concerned now. He didn't like the look of him, with his school uniform all dirty and his little pale face. 'Shall I take you home, lad?' he offered, as kindly as he could. He knew he couldn't be sitting there much longer with a small lost boy in his cab. If nothing else could be done, he would have to tell the police. As this thought crossed his mind, a constable actually started crossing the square in the direction of the hot dog stall. This gave Fergus an opportunity. 'Look, I'll go and ask that policeman if he can help you, lad.'

Suddenly: 'No! No, please mister!' came the boy's response.

*

'Why not? You'll be wanting to find your way home, won't you?'

'I'll be alright, honest!'

Fergus looked at him doubtfully, and, more out of habit than anything, he turned the pages of his newspaper and laid it aside as if nothing in it interested him. Actually, what Fergus had read in it was alarming. What he had just seen briefly sent his heart pounding. To outward appearances he was as relaxed as usual, but inside the front cover there was a clear photo of a missing boy – this boy. But what was he doing here in his cab? What was he afraid of? Fergus knocked his pipe on his heel, letting the ash fall into the road. He put the pipe on the dashboard to cool, glancing in the rear-view mirror to look at the boy again, thinking hard. 'So what are you doing here, laddie? You can't stay in my cab all day.'

The child was back crouching on the floor in the back and didn't respond. It was then an awful thought occurred to Fergus. It didn't look good. Here he was with a missing child in his cab that half of London was out looking for. He had got to get him out of there and fast. What if the policeman came over to the cab and saw the boy in there? A panic was starting up in Fergus's throat. He told himself not to be silly, felt for his leather pouch, yes, it was still there. He was sweating now, almost as if he was under attack; all this over a stupid kid that had climbed into his cab, for goodness sake!

'I...er...' Fergus began. 'Look here, Gilbert.' Somehow he didn't trust his own voice to sound as casual as it had before. 'Don't you think you'd better go now then?' he said. The question sounded a bit louder than he intended. The boy shifted his position slightly but was silent. Fergus stumbled on: 'I mean, someone will be missing you, lad - your mum or someone.'

'Mum's dead.'

'No, no, come on laddie!' Fergus sensed he was bluffing now. 'Your mum's not dead, is she?'

'And my dad!' the boy added, as if to give strength to his argument. 'I'm not going back there anyway!'

Fergus mused for a moment. The 'anyway' seemed to suggest that perhaps they weren't quite as dead as Gilbert wished they were. He was just going to ask him if he would like a lift somewhere, to a friend's house maybe, or an aunt and uncle, when the dreaded thought struck him that it might be a bad idea. Just think what it would look like, him driving along taking this boy somewhere. If the police stopped him, they'd suspect the worst. He almost felt sick at the thought.

'Well look, young Gilbert. I don't know how you got here, but I've got a home to go to and some sleep to catch up on. I've been up all night working and I'm driving again tonight. So, if you don't mind, I'll just have to say 'Cheerio'. Mind how you go now, and make sure you get home safe, OK?'

After this long speech Fergus waited for a small hand to open the cab door. 'OK? Open the door alright, can you?' He began to look forward to giving a huge sigh of relief, turning on his engine and making his usual drive back to his lodgings. As the seconds dragged past and no movement came from the back of his cab, Fergus's mind began to wander for some reason; he was back in his mother's kitchen.

She was sitting at the kitchen table and he was a small boy again, at her feet, hiding right underneath the table. There was a long tablecloth draped over it so that, when you sat under it, no one would know you were there. All kinds of things could go on, visitors came and went, grown-up's conversation that he didn't understand. Occasionally he remembered hearing his mother weeping. She often forgot he was there. Fergus felt a lump in his throat and almost choked on the vivid memory. Staggered by its realism, he jerked up his head and caught a reflection of his own face in the driver's mirror and his eyes were sore with tears. In the reflection, behind his face, the pale moon of the boy's face was watching him. Fergus saw he was looking terrified.

'You in some trouble or other, lad?' he asked, his voice quivering slightly this time. Gilbert had to answer. The question was too direct to be ignored.

'I ran away,' he said simply. 'I just run away from school, that's all.'

Back at the hot dog stall, Fergus was buying another bacon buttie and a cup of tea in a cardboard cup. His routine was well known to the stallholder. It's a wonder the other cabbies weren't about as he was usually long gone by this time, rather than hanging around his cab, buying more food and tea. He felt conspicuous, going back to his cab. The blood was rising to a crimson rash on his neck; he could feel it and he was perspiring too. 'Hell, what am I doing?' he asked himself. But still he ambled on towards the cab, carrying the bacon buttie and the tea, and realizing he hadn't said a word about the boy to the stallholder. He could have done! Why didn't he? He could have kicked himself! The stallholder could have gone and got the police, raised the alarm. But it was no use, Fergus was already there, back at the cab, handing the hot food to the hungry boy.

Gilbert began eating ravenously. As Fergus watched him, he was reminded of those Dickensian urchin boys you see on Sunday night television dramas. They devour dry bread with enormous relish and nearly drown themselves in their haste to drink. 'Mind that tea, it's hot!' he said, enjoying the brief comfort he had given the boy.

'I ran away once, stayed out all night,' Fergus told him, as he pictured his mother pleading with his father. There was drink on his dad's breath, drink on the stubble on his chin, and drink in the sweat on his brow as he towered over him. Above his head, one strong fist held the kitchen chair. 'I climbed out of the bedroom window!'

The boy leant forward, as if joining in the conspiracy. 'Yeh? Did yer get away?' cried his small eager voice.

'Yeah, I got right away lad! I did, an' I ran like hell!'

The boy laughed in delight.

How quickly you can forget fear when you're young, thought Fergus to himself. So he went on and told him the story. It had been a long old night. He had tried to shelter down at the railway station by the wagons, but it was freezing cold. And he had forgotten to put on his proper shoes: he was only wearing his slippers and they were wet through.

In the morning, he heard his father's voice talking to some of the railwaymen, so he quickly doubled back and got home to his mum before his dad did. She gave him a hot bath, crying with joy, dressed him in some warm dry clothes and swore she wouldn't let his father hit him again. Fergus looked up suddenly. He was back in the present. Gilbert had rested a small comforting hand on his shoulder.

'Best get you home now lad, eh?' he said. 'Got the address, have you?'

'Suppose so.' Gilbert took a notebook out of his blazer pocket. 'But they won't want me there, it's not my home now.'

'And why's that now?' asked Fergus, disbelieving. 'Of course they'll want you back,' he added, mentally noting that they weren't dead after all, whoever they were.

'Well let's get you home an' see, shall we?' he said. Gilbert passed the notebook to him and he read the address. There weren't many places in London he didn't know. He looked at it twice. As if to make some sense of it, he turned a few pages over, turned them back and looked at it again. Then he looked up from the notebook to the boy, who was sitting up on the back seat clutching his knees. 'This address is in Ireland, Gilbert.'

'Yeah,' the boy replied.

'I can't take you home to Ireland, Gilbert lad, now can I!' He couldn't help sounding exasperated.

'No,' came the reply. 'Anyway, I don't want to go back there,' he added, frowning.

After a while, Fergus managed to establish that the boy had run away - not from home - but from his boarding school. The name of the school he either didn't know or couldn't remember. The badge on his blazer had an emblem, a name or something on it, but it was in Latin. As he was only about eight years old, Fergus supposed it was possibly true that he didn't know the proper name or location of his school. But that didn't help Fergus. He would have to report him to the authorities after all; there was no choice in the matter. By now he was feeling terribly tired. He had been driving all night, and he wasn't thinking too clearly. What he needed to do was take another look at that newspaper article. He took a deep breath.

'So, let's play a game Gilbert,' he suggested. 'Let's pretend this cab will take you anywhere you like in the whole universe. Where would you like to go?'

Gilbert appeared to be thinking hard for a moment. 'Can I go to my gran's?' he said.

'Is that all! Oh, that doesn't sound very adventurous!' replied Fergus, cheerfully. 'And where does she live, your gran? Not in Ireland too, I hope!'

'Camden Town,' Gilbert replied without hesitating. '34 Terrace Road, Primrose Hill.'

Doing his best to disguise his relief, Fergus replied casually, 'You sound very sure of that, Gilbert. You've got a good memory, have you?'

'No, but that's where I live – well, where I used to live, 'till they sent me away to that horrible school.'

Fergus couldn't believe his luck. 'Well, if that ain't a funny coincidence,' he said. 'Camden Town, you say. So, young man, if I took you back there, you'd be alright, would yer, lad?'

'Oh yeah! Would you, mister?'

'Well, Gilbert, it's your lucky day cos that's where I was headin' straight after work later. My mother lives near there. Will your gran be at home today, do you know?'

'She's always at home,' he said with confidence. 'Gran never used to leave me on me own. She'll be there. She's always there.'

*

Feeling confident at last, Fergus turned on the ignition

and moved off into the stream of traffic. 'Right,' he said, 'we're on our way.' When they reached the junction, Fergus had an idea.

'I need to fill up with petrol, Gilbert, or neither of us will be goin' anywhere.' So he drove on a few blocks until he came to a garage, one of his usual haunts. His cab drank so much petrol, so it wouldn't hurt to top it up. When he had replaced the hose, he went inside to pay and joined the queue. He took the newspaper off the shelf by the till and flicked through it, managing to read the short article quickly before replacing it. Putting it back on the shelf, he paid for his petrol, adding a chocolate bar and a bag of crisps to the total, and, using the change, he made a couple of phone calls from the payphone. A few minutes later, he returned to the cab and they were soon back on the road again, the boy munching crisps noisily in the back.

As the autumn sun came out, they were soon passing the open spaces and trees of Regent's Park, their leaves already turning golden brown. Camden Town was ahead. Casting an eye in the rear-view mirror, he saw Gilbert sitting on the back seat looking relaxed for the first time. His keen little face had regained some of its colour, and he was gazing out of the window happily, enjoying the ride. The brief telephone call to the helpline at the end of that newspaper article had been all that was needed; the police were now informed and Gilbert's gran was expecting them in the next half-hour. Whatever the boy's problems, he hoped it could be sorted out; it's not easy, he thought to himself, being a kid.

Theresa Le Flem

A Visitor in our tool shed

There's a visitor in our tool shed
Scampering this way and that, must escape
I saw it, quick what shall I do? I scream,
Not loud. I felt ridiculous.

Myself five feet and six inches and a tiny mouse
I think it was grey but could've been brown,
So quick and so dark in our shed
It's pitch black – it's behind the dustbin

Full of garden tools – now it's in the bin
It jumped, trying to escape
Another foolish scream, why it's so small?
It's trying to get out – I want to escape

A tall adult, tiny mouse in our shed
I take tools, a fork, a spade, a rake
Cautious, but I push a heavy axe, by mistake
I don't want to harm the tiny mouse

Or do I? It's scampering around our shed
It wants an escape route
There's bird food, tulip bulb skins
They make a mess in our shed
I tip up the black dustbin, on its side
And walk the other way, quickly
Out of the door, please let it escape
I don't like it, makes me shiver

I return. There is a mouse nest
Under the spade in the dustbin
'Peter, there's a nest'
'The mouse has gone' he says

'Thank goodness, I can clean it out
Everything's clean and tidy in our shed'
Mice, for future reference
Please make your home elsewhere. Thanks.

Kate A. Harris

Clean Away

All the cleaners went away
for a marvellous training day
so very long ago
the cleaners put down their cloths
and booked a myriad minibuses
all on a holiday of their wildest dreams.
The hotels were warned well in advance
to get everything so spick and span
floors so shiny you could see your face in them
tables dust free
Back home
everything had to be done by supervisors,
managers, overseers, foremen and chargehands
While they strived,
hard-working and hard-scrubbing women
and men
lay on the sand enjoyed the sun and did almost nothing
in these latter days they smile at Mr Sheen and Mrs
Mopp
they admire well-polished floors and scrubbed down
doors
Lessons learnt
The day they carpet-burned their knees

Chris Wright

Essence of Tilly

One-eyed, low-slung, wind-driven hound
Slowly quests across the yard,
Small plump feet at the end of stumpy legs,
Head swinging from side to side,
Ears trailing, nose to the ground,
In search of food, squirrels and her mum.

Indoors, by the fire, odour of dog rises,
The acrid reek of fox's dung
Gleefully rolled in,
The dankness of damp fur
Evoking autumn leaves mulched down,
Mingling with the meaty smells of gobbled dinner.

But, drowning all, Tilly's farts,
Sulphurous, eye watering,
Stronger than curry,
The rich primordial stench of rotting swamps
Oozes across the room
In an invisible mustard cloud.

Tilly, oblivious, closes her one eye and sleeps.

Fran Neatherway

The day that changed my life

My life changed forever on Saturday morning, March 14, 2009. It was eleven years ago when an official NHS envelope plonked unexpectedly onto my doormat.

I am a Coeliac and I would like to share information on living with a strict gluten free diet.

Amazingly, one percent of the population could have Coeliac disease in the UK and sadly 70 per cent of those are estimated to be suffering undiagnosed, according to Coeliac UK.

What does it mean to be a Coeliac?

Coeliac is an auto-immune disease that you cannot catch! It is a long-term condition that does not allow gluten to be digested. Not even a crumb.

Gluten is a protein found in cereals, wheat, barley, rye and oats. It is possible to eat non-contaminated oats. It sounds crazy and means oats can be digested if they have not been grown in a field where there's been wheat, barley or rye grown. The gluten in food can cause inflammation and destruction of the lining in the small intestine.

My symptoms were typical of a Coeliac. I lost over eight kilograms in weight, looked pale and gaunt. At last I had a reason why I'd suffered bloating, an upset stomach, why I was tired all the time and generally feeling very ill.

It was six months before a diagnosis was confirmed by the consultant and doctor.

A Transglutaminase blood test for gluten showed my high level on their computers. I seem to remember it was over 100. The following blood test result, June

2009 was 64 when it should be zero! During this time, my body suffered damage as I was not absorbing essential minerals and nutrients. Without calcium, I developed osteoporosis; without iron, anaemia and lack of blood caused brain fog.

I'd had all the blood tests, including for diabetes, high cholesterol, all the personal 'nastily' invasive colonoscopy, endoscopy tests to investigate my problem and bone scans plus an abdomen x-ray. The medical bodies were efficient with their investigations.

After a large weekly shop in Tesco's, with bags of shopping spread around the kitchen and ready to put away, I opened my life-changing letter.

The letter was from my consultant with the shocking news that I was strongly coeliac.

It was upsetting that I was informed by letter at the weekend when the doctor's surgery was closed. I had to wait until Monday to see a doctor and I was impatient to discuss what the Coeliac disease meant to me and how I would have to cope with my gluten free diet. Forever.

I was angry. I had to wait until the Monday to discuss my coeliac problem with the doctor. I needed my questions answered and discover how to eat gluten free in the future.

My consultant apologised for the delay. It was suggested that I could make a complaint to the Health Authority. After a discussion with the surgery manager, I decided not to take the matter further when resources are limited, but I expressed the hope that it would not happen again.

Within two months, I put on ten pounds as gluten free foods contain high levels of sugar and fats. I had to control my constant eating when essential nutrients were not being absorbed into my body.

There isn't a cure.

I wanted to scream, 'It's not a gimmicky diet. I need gluten free foods. Forever. It's not a choice.'

Peter, my husband, consulted Google on his computer and we found all the information needed on the Coeliac UK website. There is a telephone helpline for any questions, at the end of this feature.

I felt terrible giving away all my delicious goodies containing the 'poisonous', to me, gluten.

Items including my usual biscuits, cake, pasta, crisps, sweets and a favourite, Dairy Milk chocolate never to be eaten and enjoyed again. They were given away to friends and family.

I had imagined the worst, cancer or maybe depression. I'd lost my mother on March 4, the previous year, 2008, and within three months, in June, I was made redundant from the local newspaper where I enjoyed working.

A strict gluten free diet is difficult when there is hidden gluten in many items. Sufferers need to read every label as sometimes manufacturers change their recipe and include gluten.

Somehow my gluten level is still around 20 and I have not discovered why it is still this high. All other blood tests for kidneys, liver, cholesterol, diabetes are not a problem and I continue with my strict diet.

Reading the small print on all labels is a boring task to undertake. It is worth it and at least I can control my coeliac with gluten free food and not tablets.

Over the last 11 years that I've been a coeliac, the supermarkets, shops, cafes and hotels are improving their knowledge and provision of gluten free alternatives. More supermarket shelves are stocking these special products in the Free From aisles. Sadly many of the products have a high fat and high sugar content. Maybe they will produce more savoury and healthier products in the future.

Cross contamination. Whatever does that mean?

Eating out in cafes, restaurants or hotels is embarrassing. I have to ask whether they have separate toasters for toast, clean cooking oil, and even saucepans. Any cooking preparation and utensils must not have any gluten cross contamination involved with the serving of gluten free food.

My motto when shopping or eating out is: 'If in doubt leave it out.'

A gluten intolerant or gluten sensitive condition is not as serious or long-term as the gluten does not damage the small intestine in the way it does with a Coeliac diet. However, the gluten does cause an immune response.

In our kitchen, my husband has to have a separate toaster, bread bin, and chopping board on the opposite side of the kitchen to my toaster, bread bin and chopping board. My food has to be prepared on perfectly clean food surfaces.

I felt a tremendous relief when I knew what the problem was and the gluten free diet was my new life.

It was scary. I was prescribed iron tablets to improve my anaemia, daily calcium tablets and a weekly Alendronic tablet for my developing osteoporosis. They were problems caused by gluten damaging my stomach and not allowing essential nutrients to be absorbed into my body.

Within hours of my new gluten free diet, everything changed. I felt amazingly positive, now I knew that I was a Coeliac and had to follow the gluten free diet. Before diagnosis I was trying to put on weight, I ate all day without retaining any nutrients. After giving up gluten, I needed to search for new and different gluten free products for a healthy well-balanced diet and to curb my habit of eating all day.

It's frustrating to smell the appetising aromas of my old favourite gluten containing foods, especially delicious fresh bread.

I was worried I wouldn't like the taste of my new dietary food but it is improving. We eat mostly gluten free food at home and I can share some with friends and family.

My bread certainly isn't as tasty even after eleven years. I had to move on and not be tempted by ordinary bread, cakes and biscuits. Maybe I could risk it, just a little bit? No, it would never be worth it, to be so ill again. Not ever.

I can eat a healthy diet including fish, meat, eggs, dairy products, fresh fruit and vegetables. Gluten free flour must be used when baking, making sauces or pastry. These flours can be cornflour, rice, potato, oat, nut or tapioca to list a few.

After a few months on this diet I was told I looked ten years younger! Quite a confidence boost.

At last I was given a reason why I was suffering with my symptoms.

Examples of a gluten free breakfast can include porridge and gluten free yoghurt, gluten free cereals - bran flakes, cornflakes and rice pops mixed and perhaps topped with fresh or tinned fruit for a variety of tastes and textures.

Lunch - gluten free bread, crumpets, sandwich thins with soup; a salad of lettuce, tomato, cucumber, cress and cheese, fruit, jams, marmalade. There are many choices.

Dinner - all gluten free - curries, casseroles, gluten free pasta, lasagne, meat, fish, cheese, eggs, plain meals or with gluten free sauces. Any fresh fruit, but avoid processed foods as much as possible. By adding xanthan gum and baking powder, it's possible to bake lighter tasty cakes and puddings.

I hope this is helpful whether you are a sufferer or know somebody who follows a gluten free diet.

For further information about Coeliac or gluten free symptoms, please go to your doctor or to the website for Coeliac UK.

www.coeliac.org.uk

Kate A. Harris

New Beginnings

I don't know where to start. There are so many starts in life from the arrival in a new home/town at the age of three, school, change of school, the teenage years, romances, love and marriage, travel, children, moving homes numerous times, loss of loved family, allowing the departure of children to live their own way of life (big one), loss of the love of my life, and the start of a new journey. Where to start?

Each one of these 'starts' is a chapter or book on its own. Yet how to express the sadness, the happiness, the joy, the expectation and the pleasure, and the loneliness in all these events as one start blends into the next event of the long life?

My latest start is to produce something of pleasure for someone who thinks that their life is ordinary or isn't worth sharing, because every moment is special and worthy of sharing. I don't know where this will lead me. Writing about my life adventures and joys may be an indulgence, but might lead me down a challenging path to share as a part of this anthology of stories and poems from the Café Writers authors.

And so it happened that in the midst of the turmoil of a new birth, my daughter, the loss of my mother, and joy of marriage, my husband applied for a job on an island in the Pacific Ocean. Well, when you are broke, and I mean broke, with three or four pence at the end of the week, what else do you expect? Everyone thought us mad, but we were together and so much in love. I must admit the description of our future home was a bit daunting. The interviewer had never been there so we took him at his word. A home with a straw-type roof seemed like an idyllic tropical home.

It couldn't be worse than the ground floor flat of the Victorian house we were living in. I was boiling nappies in a saucepan. No, we were ready for anything and that was what we discovered...

*

Farewelling our friends and family should have been upsetting but it was all so exciting. We were booked on the Dutch ship SS Willem Ruys sailing from Southampton in March 1960. Our belongings were crated and sent ahead to meet us on the ship. We had a month's salary in advance to buy tropical clothes (we had no money). John had been on an ocean-going liner before, but I had only been in a rowing boat on a lake!

It was huge, the cabin was spacious and there was a large Dutch cradle for Susan: at four months, she was treated with luxury, and, as for me, there was a nurse for the journey to make all her bottles and laundry. I thought I was in heaven being able to enjoy my lovely daughter without worries or work. Mind you, I was seasick for the first week and have never been able to live it down. Not a nice experience.

The food was wonderful, life on the ship was a dream and we met so many people all on an adventure for it was one of the last ships taking migrants to Australia for £10. Lots of young Irish couples were going to a new life.

En route we travelled through the Suez Canal, then Bombay, and on to Sri Lanka where we were able to explore their capital city, Singapore (then still a British colony) and on to Melbourne where we disembarked.

We spent two days there, after which we had a bit of a shock and reality hit us. We had been told that we would be on a luxury company ship. It turned out to be a Greek cargo ship. The officers were really kind, and kept apologising for the lack of amenities and I must admit it was quite difficult. Gone were my holidays, although, of course, I knew that would come to an end.

The thing I found difficult was the galley (kitchen) floor. If there were no staff on and you opened the door, the floor was black. In seconds, it changed colour as the cockroaches disappeared! Oh yes they were one-and-a-half inches long. For someone who had never seen an insect that big, it really was a shock and I was petrified for Susan. We coped for ten days. Eventually, we arrived at Nauru. John and I and another couple from England were welcomed into our new home.

First of all, we had to climb down the side of the ship after an Ellis man had taken my Susan and climbed down the ladder with her. I followed (at this point I was petrified and wondered what we were doing there). At the bottom of the ladder in the sea was a barge into which the man with my baby in his arms jumped. I had to follow suit, as did John and the other couple. The ship was anchored out at sea as it was too big for the tiny harbour. There was a cantilever on the edge of the reef which would fill the ship with phosphate and deliver to Australia, New Zealand and England. The ship would go alongside after unloading supplies for the island. Hence started a twelve-year adventure.

Pam Barton

Coffee Shop Poems #1:
The meeting at Costa

Two years after exchanging insults
in the year 11 common room,
Becky and Hugh meet by chance at Costa.
She's with her mother,
He alone.
They wait for hot drinks
and talk of old times,
how much they'd shared.

Waiting excitedly,
they discuss future plans.
Becky reveals she is going away to study.
Hugh's heart visibly sinks.
Well see you around, he finally says,
retreating to his lonely booth.

The marshmallows melt sadly in his chocolate.
She sips her frothy latte,
the taste lingering in her mouth.

John Howes

Coffee Shop Poems #2: Monday morning

Monday morning in the shopping centre,
the grey gloom presses in
depressing me,
old people shuffle round with carrier bags and minimal
greetings.
'Did you see *Central News*?'
'No, we watch the BBC.'
The *Daily Mail* glares up from the table
beckoning the unsuspecting into its lair of disgust.
My coffee, my weapon against the dismal
then
the car radio lifts me out of the cesspool.
Bach whirls me into the stratosphere of life.

The world keeps turning -
    just

John Howes

Coffee Shop Poems #3:
The couple

Why don't they speak?
He says nothing, she says nothing.
They stare at the dreary rain,
The parking cars,
The Christmas shoppers.

I search for that comfortable silence
Between old friends and lovers
But find none.
Not even a crossword can bring them together.

As they drink up,
Did I see an accidental touch?
Or was it a brush of hands
That meant
We love each other beyond words.
All has been said already.

John Howes

Mynhath's Harvest

'Please, Mynhath, we need to leave now; it will soon be dusk, and we have to get back,' said Eydearthe, my maid, her eyes scanning the horizon.

'It's okay, we won't be long; I just want to make sure that Geoffrey has laid the correct drainage channels.'

But as I got up, brushing the dirt from my dress, a little girl of about eight years, one of the young children who had been following us, handed me a necklace of buttercups and daisies; she smiled shyly at my grin of gratitude then became embarrassed, turning away, whispering something in Eydearthe's ear.

'What did she say, Eydearthe?' I asked.

Eydearthe's face lit up in a big smile. 'She said you are a beautiful woman, my Lady, and very kind.'

Now I felt embarrassed, not only because Eydearthe had called me 'My Lady', but also because of being reminded of my looks. Like Eydearthe, I was very tall, just over six feet, and, like all our people, we were very good looking, with blue-grey eyes that glittered with brightness. The Saxons and Normans assumed that we were Norse or Danes, but we had come from much further away. Earlier, I had seen my reflection in the village pond and, now over three hundred years old, I still looked as if I was in my mid-twenties to these people, but I had also noticed that I had aged slightly over the last seven years whilst living on this planet of earth and water.

On our own world, everyone was equal and, although I was one of fifty-three elected Councillors, the title did not carry any particular special status or privilege; it merely meant that I had to manage duties carrying out the will of our people. Eydearthe, my closest friend from childhood days, had been my constant companion, so when the chance came to carry out a harvest, we naturally went together.

Chosen to lead the harvest expedition, I had set off with a team of eighteen women. On our world, all citizens were female but to supplement our numbers, every ten years, we harvested suitable males from this planet of earth and water.

When the harvest was completed and the seed taken, after one full moon cycle of our planet, the males' recent memories were wiped, and they were returned to their planet. In this way, we kept our numbers up and introduced fresh stock into our genes.

Our present journey had coincided with England's King Edward I's reign in the latter part of their thirteenth century. We always had a good idea of where to go and where the best opportunities would arise to obtain suitable stock; to that end, an advance party had located assorted venues and I had then been selected to lead the harvest collection. Arriving in orbit on this planet of earth and water, I separated us into nine teams of two, each team analysing and evaluating the target stock; only fit specimens would be selected with the final choosing married with character and intelligence.

Our world had survived for thousands of years and we didn't want to jeopardise our future by selecting a bad seed. I had chosen two parties to work the territories in England, the other seven parties sent elsewhere on the planet. On completion of selection, the nominated targets were gathered, the stock being stored on the mother craft, which would then return home.

The reason I had chosen two parties for the English territory was because not only did they provide men of hard work and chivalry, but also because their King was involved in conflicts in the neighbouring territories of Wales, Scotland, and France, which meant that men disappearing during that period did not elicit undue enquiry.

But then I had fallen down on my mission. With the end in sight I had attended a medieval joust because I was intrigued regarding the mock fighting entertainment and I had also been drawn to a certain name who was on the list of harvest candidates. He was tall, young, and brown-haired with blue eyes. Something about his demeanour, his character, just roped me in; the locals used the word chivalrous and, whatever that was, I liked it. He was also strong and intelligent and seeing how he interacted with his peers, particularly the females, I was fascinated. I had also become aware of the close relationships between certain men and women, the fondness and affection that they showed to each other and I felt a longing, a sadness within me.

The man I had come to admire was called Godfrey; it transpired that he was a Lord and had inherited a large tract of land in the north of the country. He had three Vassal Lords, innumerable serfs, and feudal territory including several villages as well as manor houses and a large castle. But I didn't know that at the time; I was more infatuated with the man, not the wealth.

Our quotas were getting full, the potential stock nearly completed – in fact some of the teams had already returned to the mother craft with their selections – but I didn't want to go until the end of the tournament. Godfrey was high on my list and I wanted to wait, fascinated to find out if he would become the eventual winner of the jousting. Twice each day, he had entered the arena, mounted on his Destrier, an enormous horse covered in an azure blue coat trimmed with gold chevrons, the same colours that Godfrey wore, except that Godfrey also had a black boar emblem emblazoned on his shield and on the left side of his tunic.

He had remained undefeated over the first two days; it was now the third day and there was a final joust to take place. Eydearthe and I were sure that Godfrey would win so we settled down from our observation point to watch the final encounter.

The Nobility had taken their seats, the serfs and peasants standing apart in fenced-off enclosures. There was a sense of anticipation, jollity, excesses of eating and drinking, but also there was a certain sense of the macabre, some of the peasants hoping against hope that one of their Vassals or Lords would incur a serious injury.

I had enjoyed the previous days' spectacles, the jousting had been competitive, without serious injury, and in the evenings, the nobility celebrated to excess, with the serfs and peasants also enjoying time from work, ale and surplus food finding its way to their cloth-covered straw bales.

And then it had happened. Whether from excess mead the night before or whether it was because his opponent's horse partially slipped just before contact, Godfrey's lance caught in his competitor's stirrup causing the other knight's stallion to rear, front hooves kicking up in the air. The opposing knight's lance skidded against Godfrey's shield, tearing free a strip of the iron that had been used to band the edges, sharp metal caught on the lance point spearing into Godfrey's head.

He fell, tumbling across the wooden partition, the loud crack of breaking bones heard as he dropped, first against the wood, then on impact onto the hard ground, a cloud of displaced earth and grass rising into the air before returning gently to earth.

I cried out in anguish, momentarily oblivious to our mission, then put my hand to my mouth, ducking down just before heads turned to look where Eydearthe and I were perched atop a stable block. Eydearthe gave me a stern look, her reprimand needing no words. I had nearly broken the first rule of our harvests - never expose ourselves to the natives.

Fortunately, my shriek was quickly forgotten; we had not been noticed, the tournament crowd more interested at the sight in front of them, eyes focused on the gory vision of the broken, bleeding, fallen knight.

There was a general murmur of regret from most in the crowd, with quite a few wails of anguish and regret from some of the females; Godfrey had been their favourite and now there was only desolation left. The tournament winner accepted his victory with embarrassment, a jeer from the onlookers not helping, but the prize money soon wiped the awkwardness from his visage, a huge smile of triumph lighting up his sweat-covered, grimy face.

Godfrey's body was dragged from the field, his Squires being as gentle as possible; two females in all their finery weeping copiously as they walked by his side.

I had turned to Eydearthe, 'What a shame; he was one of the better ones,' and strangely, I had a tear in my eye.

'That's how it goes sometimes,' she had replied dismissively, 'Now we need to arrange uplift of the chosen ones, then I shall be glad to get home.' She scrambled down from the roof, a young boy standing open mouthed as he watched this lady revealing more than she should.

'Wait for me,' I had called out, before making my way down in a more decorous fashion.

We returned to our craft which was camouflaged in the woods and meticulously compiled the final numbers. Within two hours the collection had been made, and it was the turn for Eydearthe and me to return to the mothership. But I could not remove the image from my mind of the broken Godfrey, the regret from all who knew him, and the weeping and wailing that was still coming from his tent, mourning for his imminent death.

Eydearthe knew me too well; she could see the look in my face. 'You can't,' she said. 'It's against all our rules. We can't take him, we only take fit stock.'

The look on my face did not change.

'Oh Mynhath, you're not serious, you can't be? The medical treatment to fix him on this planet will not be available for hundreds of years, if at all. It would not be accepted by the Council or any of us. We can take stock, but we can't interfere in their progress.'

I had grimaced.

'Oh, for Queen's sake,' she had retorted, resigned that my mind was made up.

We waited for another hour until only one Squire and a weeping female remained; I sent in Eydearthe with a sleeping draught and the distraught duo, thirsty and miserable, had soon drunk sufficiently to knock themselves out. With Eydearthe's help I had carried Godfrey to our craft and, with the aid of the medical computers, had found the necessary answers of how to fix him. The medical procedure, including mending the bones, would take up to thirty hours.

Then the mother craft contacted us, asking what the delay was. I misled them, advising that I had been given another task by the Council before leaving our world, and that there would be a slight delay; as I was disconnecting our communication I could hear the loud sound of multiple grumbling.

Encasing Godfrey in a container, a loose-fitting medical suit, we fitted a breathing mask, then filled it with medical fluid. With the procedure from the computer analysis, I programmed the container with the data necessary to mend Godfrey. Eydearthe and I had then sat down, eaten a quick meal, then fallen asleep almost immediately; it had been a long day.

I had been woken by a large humming noise which grew louder and more insistent. Confused as to where I was, it took a few moments for my brain to defog. I cleared my head and then pressed the control to raise my pilot's seat, which had been fully reclined. Glancing at Eydearthe, I could see that she was still fast asleep, her gentle breathing undisturbed by the incessant humming of our communications. Reluctantly, I pressed the open communication control for I knew it was not going to be good news. I was correct; we were now overdue, the mother craft being ordered home immediately. Checking the time-piece, I noted that it had been twelve hours since we had started the medical procedure, with another eighteen still needed. It was no good pleading with the vessel or with my home world for I knew within my heart that we had to leave now. The journey home would only just get us back in time for the commencement of the fertility cycle.

If I had not interfered Godfrey would already have been dead, but, if I left now, I was condemning the man to life as a cripple, because although the healing process had begun, his spine and damaged bones had yet to correctly re-form.

Eydearthe had woken and was staring up at me, her eyes knowing, a fear crossing her face. 'You surely can't, Mynhath, you can't stay on this planet; not only are they barbaric, this land of earth and water is ruled solely by men.'

'I know, Eydearthe, but what can I do? I started the healing process and if I leave him now it will be much worse for him than if he had died. Leave me with the medical container and you take our craft back.'

'I have never left you on your own and will not start now. If you stay, I stay.'

We removed the container and, making our apologies and saying our farewells to the crew, we sent our craft to the mothership; I re-allocated command to Synrega who was the next natural leader.

Returning with Eydearthe to Godfrey's tent, we located a bemused Squire, wondering where the body of his dead Lord had gone. His senses had still been confused from the sleeping draught so it was an easy task to inform him that I was a medical woman from the Norse lands, and that I could save his Lord's life, restoring him to full health. I explained that we needed to take him away, and that he was already loaded into a 'box'. With the Squire's help, we had located a wagon and two oxen, Godfrey's container loaded up, and we had set off, at a very gentle pace, to Godfrey's castle in the North.

By the time we arrived at the castle, the thirty hours had passed, but I did not want to open the container in a public area. Resisting protests from Godfrey's castle stewards, I instructed Squires to carry the container to Godfrey's quarters. It was then that I opened the container, Godfrey slowly wakening, his eyes, at first unfocused, then fixing on me. Our eyes stayed locked for innumerable minutes, something strange passing between us, and from that day on we have never been apart.

Together for seven blissful years, with the knowledge, intelligence and experience that Eydearthe and I had, Godfrey's feudal lands had become the most fertile and productive in the whole of King Edward's territories. There had been initial resistance from the Vassal Lords and their serfs, but our methods were quickly proven and finally accepted. Even the serfs were happier compared with their previous existence, living better and freer lives than they had been under the feudal system introduced by the Norman Conqueror; it was almost like the old days.

However, our success caused resentment from other Lords and Barons, particularly our adjacent landowner, Baron Robert, a rapacious bear of a man, built like an ox and with a fiery temper. Robert had fought as a Norman mercenary with Byzantium forces in the Balkans and against invading Islamist forces from Asia, his blood-thirsty deeds being proudly recounted during the many indulgent feasts that he organised, boasting arrogantly to anyone who would hear of his nefarious deeds. But as fast as he profited from the spoils of war, the quicker he got through it - whoring, drinking, gambling, and eventually making enemies of his Byzantium paymasters. Fortunately for Robert, but not for Godfrey and me, Robert's older brother died, so Robert determined to come to England and take care of his brother's family.

Taking care of the family was Robert's way of gaining control; he forced the widow to marry him, his nephew dying a mere few months later of a stomach ailment which we are sure was caused by poison. Thus, Robert inherited everything, but his lifestyle and greed was soon draining the property's coffers. My husband Godfrey and I had attended one of Robert's banquets, but the Baron Robert was such an obnoxious bore, vain and uncouth, that we determined not to socialise again.

My thoughts were brought back to the here and now, Eydearthe was right, the daylight was fading. Bidding farewell to Geoffrey, one of my husband's three Vassal Lords, I suddenly noticed smoke on the horizon, not the faint smoke from a hamlet, no, it was something much greater, a large cloud that could only be caused by a major fire.

'Something's wrong,' I called out to Eydearthe. 'Look; it must be a great fire, in the direction of the castle.'

Almost instantly a rider appeared on the horizon, then rode down from the hilltop, his horse's pace frantic, the animal almost frothing, the rider leaning in the saddle as if weighed down by a great weight. My heart froze, a sixth sense telling me that something evil was happening.

Geoffrey sent one of his warriors to intercept the incoming rider, and grabbing the incoming man's reins, he slowed the wildly cantering horse, bringing horse and rider to us. The rider was barely alive, an arrow shaft sticking from his back, a bloody gash splitting his head from left ear to his neck. That he was still alive was some kind of miracle, and slowly raising his head, he mumbled, 'I'm so sorry, my Lady; Lord Godfrey sent me to warn you not to return home.' Then he went quiet, and I thought he had died but his body twitched slightly, his breathing shallow and weak.

'Help him down, and give him some water,' I ordered, and two other warriors assisted him down from his horse, laying him gently on his side on the ground. I recognised him as one of my husband's household warriors, Aylwin.

Cupping his head under my left hand, I gently gave him a few drops of water. Pulling the arrow free would probably kill him, so one of Geoffrey's warriors cut the tip free, and if we could stabilise Aylwin, then there was a chance that I could remove the arrowhead and remaining part of the arrow from his body later.

Aylwin's eyes opened, shock and pain etched on his face. 'My Lady,' he wheezed, repeating, 'Lord Godfrey says you are not to return.' Pausing, sucking in more air, he rattled, 'Baron Robert, supported by other Vassal Lords, has attacked us, burnt the village outside the castle, killed our men and taken the castle. He came with a small party to negotiate the purchase of grain; it was a trick, his war force hiding in wagons supposedly to take the grain home.'

Anger flared within me and I almost let Aylwin's head drop to the ground as I began to rise before dropping back to my knees.

'Oh Mynhath,' Eydearthe spoke softly, her hand resting comfortingly on my shoulder, 'I'm so sorry.'

'Lord Godfrey? My children?' I snapped unkindly at Aylwin.

It took a few seconds before his eyes opened again, the pain obviously driving through his nerves, trying to tear his soul free.

'Lord Godfrey was mortally wounded…dying,' he wheezed, 'The children taken; I was ordered to tell you to flee.' The effort for Aylwin was too much, my determination and anger to get quick answers dragging the last ounce of energy from the man. He sucked in air one more time, then died, a foul stench of breath being expelled as the air finally left his broken body.

Rising to my feet, I clenched my fists in anger, a fire burning in my eyes. On my world I had been trained as a warrior, and although we were all equal, many of us had been trained in warfare; it was a necessity for we never knew if some other off-world force would view us as rich pickings. We were always ready to defend what was ours, and the warrior blood ran through my veins. Robert would pay, and I would free my children, a little boy of almost six years, Wydo, and a girl of three, Estrid. I had produced them and given birth to them unlike the system that we used on our world; also, on our world we had never kept boys older than two, but I loved Wydo as much as Estrid.

'Sir Geoffrey,' I demanded of my husband's Vassal, 'How many men can you give me?'

Geoffrey hesitated awkwardly, regretfully replying, 'Only ten my Lady, the rest of my warriors are fighting with the King's army in Wales.'

'Bloody King Edward,' I thought, remembering also that our other two Vassal Lords, and their warriors, were fighting with Edward's forces. Godfrey had even sent most of our own men because King Edward needed additional fighters to subdue the Scots whilst still conquering the Welsh lands. We were thin on the ground with remaining warriors and maybe it would be only the three of us, plus Geoffrey's ten, but I would not run. It was my home, my children.

As much as Geoffrey was reluctant to take our minimum force into combat, he was loyal to Godfrey and would do his duty. 'You stay here, my Lady,' he declared bravely. 'I'll take my men and see what can be done.' He turned away calling his men to arms, but I called him back.

'No, Sir Geoffrey, I am coming too; do you have leather and armour that will fit?'

Geoffrey looked at me doubtfully. 'I don't believe so, Lady Mynhath, and I don't think it would be wise.'

'Don't tell me that!' I snapped at him. 'I can fight as well as most men, and by God, I will avenge my husband.' There was a fire in my belly that I had never known before. 'Get me a sword and some armour or chainmail; *now!*'

Geoffrey was taken aback, both by my tone and being ordered at by a woman.

I threw Eydearthe's restraining hand from my arm, glared at her in anger, the words forming on her lips instantly stifling, and then faced back to Geoffrey who had remained stationary. The look on his face made me realize how harsh my words had been, and I felt very foolish.

'I'm so sorry, Sir Geoffrey; I should not have spoken so to such a person who has shown great allegiance to my family, but I am in grief and anger, and I am not sure which emotion is running stronger within me.'

'Exactly!' retorted Eydearthe. 'We need to be rational.'

'You can be as rational as you want, but I am going

back.' My tone was harsher than I meant it to be, but I was determined, my mind fixed on a mixture of revenge for my husband and to rescue my two children. 'Whether I go on my own or with any of you, the choice is entirely yours.' I looked around in defiance at those standing around me.

John, a cripple, his bad leg dragging behind him, stepped forward. 'I will go my Lady, I can use my staff.' And he waved it in the air almost toppling over, the wooden staff no longer supporting his weight.

I smiled at John, now feeling foolish. 'Thank you, John, but I am afraid Robert's men would cut you down in seconds.' Disappointed, he limped away, a brave man, one of Geoffrey's serfs who had seen battle twenty years ago.

'Of course, my men and I will go, my Lady,' Geoffrey replied sadly, knowing that it may be the end for him as well. 'We will not have any armour that will fit you...or your maid,' he glanced at Eydearthe. 'But I'm sure that we can find some leather jerkins and chainmail, and perhaps helmets, to fit.' He set off to look for any protection that he could find for us and to organise our small war party.

'I guess that means I'm coming too,' sighed Eydearthe.

I looked at her coldly. 'You don't have to; this is my war.'

'We have always stood together, and I'm not leaving you now. Besides, if something happens to you, I don't want to be the only one of my kind on this planet.' Her expression was fixed, eyes challenging, yet accusing.

I stared at her for a moment, then realized how ridiculous and selfish I was being. 'I'm sorry for everything I have put you through on this planet, and sorry that you have not experienced the joys that I have, the love, a husband, the children, so please don't get yourself killed on my behalf. Find shelter, a convent, where you can hide until the next harvest comes from our world.'

Eydearthe smiled. 'I may not have had the joys that you have had, but I have enjoyed every day on this planet of earth and water; it has been so different to our world, and so many varieties of things to do. I would not have changed it, but I confess that I would not be happy on my own.'

We embraced and were still embracing when Geoffrey returned with assorted clothing that might fit us. Awkwardly, we separated, and retired to one of the peasant's hovels where we tried on the various options given. After a few minutes, we both emerged, looking ridiculous in our ill-fitting wardrobe. Neither of us had armour but, importantly, we both were wearing a suit of chainmail over a leather jerkin and leather trouser, which although not as effective as armour, would afford some protection.

When we rode over the horizon, I could see the flames from my castle climbing into the sky, and my heart sank, a heavy weight growing in my stomach. Approaching closer, I saw Godfrey's body, hanging limply from one of the battlements, the village surrounding our home burning furiously in a sea of flame and smoke. Older women were staggering around, confused, directionless, lost as if they were souls from hell, wailing, crying for their dead menfolk. What men there had been lay strewn across the ground, most stripped of their chainmail and weapons, and even their shoes, their bodies left in a bloody mess, a frenzied mass of merciless killings.

Losing all sense of reason, I urged my horse forward, charging like a Berserker, the very sort of person whose seed our world had never chosen because of their mad, reckless, and blood-thirsty behaviour.

Eydearthe tried to restrain me but it was futile; I was off, the warriors following my gallop.

I charged under the open portcullis and through the gate, my small fighting force following, a scene of destruction and mayhem hitting my eyes. Most of the wooden buildings were smouldering wrecks, and Baron Robert's men were either standing around, drinking ale, glorifying in their success or else raping the younger Saxon women that they had taken.

Although all our fighting men had obviously been killed resisting the raiders, judging by their positions in death, some had been executed after surrendering. Our fighters' bodies were splattered from just inside the gatehouse all the way to the main Keep.

There were also quite a few of Robert's men no longer able to breathe on this planet; so even though taken unawares, our forces had put up a good fight. It was evident that Robert had recruited other forces, because I quickly worked out that there were at least fifty men milling within the grounds with probably many more inside the Keep.

All this I took in within seconds, my sword loose from its scabbard as I attacked, hacking defenceless men left and right, and then parrying, defending, thrusting at those who started retaliating. I was bloodthirsty, relentless, ignorant of what was happening to my force behind.

We were like madmen, the opposition warriors

caught unawares, as no doubt they had done to my beloved Godfrey when they had attacked our castle. Robert's men were in disarray but then a trumpet sounded, and his forces withdrew, defending themselves as they backed off. I foolishly thought that the tide had turned and that the day was now in our favour. Reining in my horse, I glanced behind me, seeing that only seven of us remained. My dear Eydearthe was not amongst us. Turning my horse, an arrow whistled past my head, a flight of arrows following instantly thereafter; two arrows hit my horse, the poor creature snorting in pain, its legs buckling, and we fell together, my horse trapping my right leg.

I looked on helplessly as my remaining men were struck down one by one; I was a warrior and would not cry but my heart went out for their souls. It was all over very quickly; those men who had not died from their wounds were quickly dispatched, their throats cut, our dear warriors gurgling in their death throes as their blood fell to the ground. I turned my head away.

When I looked up, Baron Robert was standing over me, a gloating smile on his face. 'Take her to my new bedchamber,' he smiled, 'But don't harm her. When I have finished with her, then you can do what you like.'

Locked in the room that used to be my bedroom, my emotions finally overtook me, and I wept like never before. Now I remembered why we were a world of women only; men had always wanted more. Never satisfied, they had coveted their neighbours' properties and possessions.

The sensible women had formed a Council and after a long conflict, men had been driven from our world; they are still out there somewhere, with a handful of our women who left with them, no doubt still fighting and squabbling amongst themselves.

The key turned in the lock and the door slowly opened. I searched for any weapon determined that I would not be taken easily, my heartbeat rapid, blood rushing in my ears, and then I emitted a sigh of relief; it was Eydearthe, wounded, the upper part of her left arm encased in a bloody bandage. And she was with Estrid, my daughter's tiny hand in Eydearthe's hand. I almost cried out in ecstasy, then looked behind her for Wydo.

Eydearthe shook her head sadly. 'He was outside, playing with the local boys; they were amongst the first to be killed.'

I cried again whilst rushing to embrace Estrid.

'Quickly,' interrupted Eydearthe. 'We can escape through the rear gatehouse; Robert's men are busy getting drunk, celebrating their victory, and have left it unguarded.'

Stealthily, we made our way through the castle, out from the rear gatehouse, and finding two tethered horses, we galloped away into the night.

'We go west,' I announced. 'To the land of the Irish, and will join a convent. In three years, the next harvest will visit this planet and I still have our communication device.' I fingered the brooch that I had taken from my room. 'Then we will go home, to sanity and sanctuary.'

With heavy hearts we rode on into the hills, westward, the day's dusk falling into a black, moonless night.

*

A discarded shield moved, a young face peering from underneath. It was quiet, the murder and chaos over. Wydo climbed to his feet, taking in everything that was still visible from the dying flames.

This part human, mainly alien child, knew he had to leave, but he would be back. The human part would require vengeance.

Desmond B. Harding

The Stone Balancer

'I love my love with an R because he is radical,' Alice exclaimed. 'I hate him with an R because he is... ruthless!'

'It's your turn, Mum. Oh, come on, join in!' Debbie said.

'Not now,' I snapped, and stomped down the lane, resisting the temptation to put my fingers in my ears. Their endless quoting from *Pirates of the Caribbean* yesterday had been bad enough. But I knew I shouldn't get so het up. There were far worse things for thirteen-year olds to be keen on than Victorian word games.

The lane crossed a wide stream. As I waited for them to catch up, I leaned on the parapet of the bridge and gazed at the bright foliage reflected in the chestnut brown water murmuring below.

'What're those?' Alice said. She pointed to several tall piles of stone that broke the rippling water.

'Let's go and have a look. We could paddle!' Debbie said.

'No,' I said. 'We've only been walking an hour. We were late starting, thanks to you two reading *Lord of the Rings* until midnight and then having to be dragged out of bed!'

'Yeah, I know, but, pleeeease?'

The stream looked cool, the line of miniature stone towers intriguing.

'Well...all right. But only for a few minutes!'

We tossed our rucksacks, boots and socks onto the shingle. I wriggled my bare toes in the cold water. It felt like iced tonic bubbling over my pummelled feet. We had had five wonderful days walking Hadrian's Wall, the switchbacks and views of the central section had been glorious, but this moment would be up there with the best, I decided.

The girls laughed, splashed and exclaimed, 'They're weird!' at the stone towers. Suddenly a huge, bearded man came round a corner and strode downstream towards us. He had sploshing, khaki waders and a misshapen hat. He paused, stared, then threw his arms wide.

'So you like my stone balancing!' he roared. 'Most walkers march past with their heads down. They never even look. But you – you stopped!'

'These are yours?' Alice asked.

'Aye!' he said, as he strode up to us.

'Why?'

'Tis but an idle fancy,' he said, crouched down and whispered to her, 'But mayhap... tis a boundary for the fair folk.'

He straightened up and winked at me.

'Can we make one?' Debbie said.

The four of us found and balanced several flat stones into a satisfying but precarious turret. I glanced at my watch.

'Time to go,' I said, reluctantly.

As we waved goodbye, he said, 'May good fortune speed you on your way!' then splashed back upstream.

'Tom Bombadil!' Alice exclaimed, with round eyes. 'We've met Tom Bombadil!'

Maybe we had. Whoever he was, he had refreshed us and it no longer mattered to me that we were two hours behind schedule. We'd get there.

'Come on, girls,' I said, striding up the lane. 'My

turn! Right. I love my love with an S because he is, er, savoury!'

'Go Mum!' Debbie cheered.

Cathy Hemsley

The Boy With The Kite

The boy with the kite
Out on the estuary sands
A lone figure battling the wind
And ignoring the rain

The nylon fabric cracks
And the taut line sings
As the kite strives to break away
Driven by the wind

The boy doesn't notice the rain
Or the biting cold
On his face, concentration,
And a quiet smile

Is he up there with the kite?
As it dips and turns circles
Under his control
Is he flying too?

The boy with the kite
On the estuary sands

E. E. Blythe

A Ruined City's Lament

Through crumbled rock-strewn streets
I hear the earth itself cry out:

Rubble, rubble, fruit of trouble,
Rise up, be strong and stand your ground!
Be strengthened now, restore yourselves
your walls, your coverings, your roofs, rebuild!
Let craters deep be filled, let floors be cleared,
stand up your doors and oil your locks
Rooms, temples, harbours, schools
Protect your citizens from war
or else be warned
the children you once homed
will all be gone

Sand of the desert sun, restore yourself!
Stones of the ancient days, be tall again!
Repel the bombs, reject their ammunition
Look! Your people need your tough protection
Don't lie in ruins so, rise up, be brave
and shelter those you loved before
or to be sure
when next those evil ones take aim and fire
the people you once homed
will all be gone

Theresa Le Flem

Shells

We live in a restaurant aquarium
Not very happy someone ordered Mum
Me you and in a prison cell
Ignoring the bouillabaisse smell
Armour against a sea of troubles
Hiding in the constant bubbles
We're all stuck in a shell
Strapped on tightly to the carousel
Eggs served up to fate
Cracked passed our best by date??
For assistance
this instance

A man once loved a goddess in a game of light
played that Wii day and night
Get off that screen it's doing you no good
Moss-side decaying like rotten wood

The bubble you love so much
a comfort and a crutch
we see so much and hear you talk
I'll take you on an eggshell walk …
candy crush
sugar rush
Jesus Christ
Mum's advice
petrol head
lost war dead
Ronnie Biggs, Nigel Farage
hugs, romance, lust, love and marriage

Joseph Smith's scrappy book
Robert Smith's gothic look
Will Smith the fresh prince
Patti Smith; Sam makes me wince
DIY cathedrals
Plato polyhedrals
family history
UFO mystery
soap opera drudgery
selling Devon fudgery
liberating Palestine
punting on the Serpentine
fracking, runways, HS2
poetry and the thing you do
Monty Python Mr Bean
Bonar Colleano and God Save the Queen

Once Two crabs in a Paris tank
Pets of choleric chef Frank
Served in error by a waiter
Rasped to death with the cheese grater

The hermit crab is saved from the pan
Change your shell as often as you can

Chris Wright

At The Hospital

I'm at the hospital, in a consulting room.
It's hot and clammy. The windows are sealed tight.
I'm facing a senior consultant and a fifth-year medical
student.
They stare at me intently. Slowly, as if with forceps, my
symptoms are dragged out of me.
'Well, yes, so what if I get up at night to pee? Doesn't
everybody?'
'Is there a dribble after I finish?'
'How the hell should I know? It's dark.'
'What about my rate of flow? What?!'
Shall I tell them about the blood in my poo?
'Of course I smoke! Doesn't everybody?'
'Exercise? What are you talking about! I'm retired!'
'Eating habits! What's wrong with pizza and chips?'
And chips wouldn't be chips without whiskey.
And whiskey wouldn't be whiskey without a large one.
'How large?' she asks plaintively.
'How large is the glass?' I reply.
'I'm 69 years old. My name is Mr Ben Wright.'
(They have to get this bit right or they fail.)
The medical student scribbles furiously and with effort.
The pen shatters under pressure from her index finger.
She looks at me, I look at her.
I blink my eyes downwards.
Now she gets the message.
She now examines my medical notes in minute detail.
The consultant looks at me sadly from behind lowered
spectacles.
He says nothing.

The student starts to give her appraisal in front of me as if I'm no longer there.
The word carcinoma lights up the room like a Christmas tree.
Then she leaves and we discuss her body language and general manner.
And I award a sequence of marks from the sheet before me.
Me with one O-level in Sociology grading final year medical students!
An actor!
You see, I'm here for a week of role play and fortunately that's all it is.
I've memorised the script intently and learnt to repeat it verbatim throughout the day.
Five times every hour.
Word perfect without deviation or repetition.
And throughout the day my mind is cross referencing and thinking.
Never mind the role play, these symptoms, they're mine.
I do get up to pee.
I'm doomed. That carcinoma, it's mine. I have only days to live.
I break out in a sweat.
Another candidate enters the room.
I commence my spiel but it's after lunch and difficult to concentrate.
I look again at this new student doctor.
She turns her head towards me with that sudden sheath of auburn hair bursting across her shoulders. The room moves into soft focus.
I'm back at school on the rickety swaying bus, taking us back after a netball victory.
The atmosphere is high on adrenaline and toilet rolls

are being thrown from the back windows.

I'm having my first kiss with Maxine Daybourgh. She leans in towards me.

It's hot, sticky and sudden. Lips pursed, breaking towards each other.

Others start to cheer.

But I know in my heart of hearts she only did it 'cos I paid her.

It's a romance I can't afford to sustain.

But here's the critical thing:

My humiliation a week later, glimpsed from behind the blazers in the cloakroom.

At 4 o'clock by the water fountain, she kissed Michael Dobbs for nothing.

And not just once either. Jezebel!

Her face drifts out of view and I'm back with the examination.

Two people stare at me with forensic intensity.

The student and the consultant.

The atmosphere is tense. The air seems to have been sucked out of the room, as if we have decompression.

Where have I been? Have I mentioned blood in the poo?

Have I mentioned smoking?

Have they mentioned the haemoglobin count?

Which bit are we at now?

Later that same day. The student in front of me is wearing a hijab and speaks so softly we can hardly hear her.

Her eyes are averted and she peers at the ground.

'Describe from the chart before you what you see.'

'There is discolouration and blurring, this may well be a carcinoma'.

'And your other prognosis might be?'

'A benign prostatic hypertrophy including OAB.'

But that perfume she's wearing. Just a hint of winter
mist.
Suddenly, I'm four years old and in the back garden of
the big house in Ipswich.
I'm rolling under a hedge and there, just out of reach, is
my sister's christening mug. Paper thin silver and with
embossed hieroglyphics.
I'm too young to read.
My fingers explore inside the mug. I smell wood,
bracken and leaves.
But most of all I smell dampness.
I peer inside and a grey black snail crawls towards me.
I'm jolted back into the examination room.
The student has left.
'And did she ask for your name correctly?'
I glance across at the examiner.
She is asking for my confirmation.
She comes from Felixstowe, flies to Croatia for Christian
Aid and is married to an accountant called Ray. She met
him after ten years of being single. She was married to
medicine, until she met Ray.
They have two children.
'And did she ask for your name correctly?'
I haven't a clue. I can't remember a thing.
Suddenly the entire future career of this year five
student hangs in the balance, because of me.
This is an Objective Structured Medical Examination.
It's called an OSME.
And it's a re-sit.
Did she? I think she did.
'Yes,' I say with unblemished authority.
'She did.'
'You're certain?'
'Oh yes.'

She scribbles a mark on the paper before her.
I follow suit with a string of ticks.
It's the 33rd person of the day.
Finito.
I struggle to the canteen to meet my fellow thespians.
How Shakespeare would have laughed.
Poor Claire has had nothing but manic depression all day.
'And last week it was a still-born child, all bloody week!'
Jerry's overjoyed. He's had acute diabetes and alcohol abuse.
'Nice change from dementia and arthritis.'
Jerry, the only man I know who's had his face on the back of a bus!
David's been down with diverticulitis.
'I don't know what it means but what a great word.'
He rolls the sound around his tongue like a boiled sweet.
We all know him as Inspector Pluto, the psychic detective.
As seen on Channel 12.
But Queen of the Daisies?
Eileen.
But we are all envious of Eileen. An examination for rectal cancer has meant lying in bed all day, being poked.
Money for old rope, we say.
Money for old rope.

Simon Grenville

Elegy for a dead warrior

It has come. The day I never thought to see. My friend is dead.

We were of an age, but I thought I would be the first to go. Not him, so strong and vital.

We talked when he passed through Ely, a few brief days ago. We spoke of old times, a little about the battle to come, but nothing of the future. We both knew the truth; that he would die. It was his time.

I followed behind the battle host. They moved fast, eager for the fight. I brought a slow cart, with which to carry his body home.

Now it is finished. The sea wolves have gone, their boats sliding away, back to the sea. Triumphant but sorely depleted. They will not be back again this year. Perhaps next, but who will there be to send them home then, now he is dead?

He did his duty, now I must do mine. The field is wide. The earth cut and bloodied from the fight. The smell of blood and death overwhelms me. There are others, searching for friends and relatives, hoping against hope that they will find a living body and not a corpse. Some perhaps look for plunder. They will look in vain; the victors will have taken everything of value.

It is difficult to walk. I slip and fall to my knees. As I struggle to stand, the body beside me moves. Is he alive still? No. Just the tug on his scattered guts that gave him the semblance of life and like a child's toy, he drops back to his everlasting sleep. I sketch a cross above his body and move on. The coarse wool of my cassock feels damp against my legs. At least the blood, and worse, will not show against the black Benedictine cloth. As I try to identify the lines of battle, the world turns red. The sky reflects the blood spilled on the ground below. The sun sinks towards the nearby town, set upon its hill. Flat land and water surround it. Ahead the island floats; separate, for now, from the land. That must be where the bridge joined it to this land, for there is the greatest spread of bodies.

As I approach, I recognise some faces, or if they have no faces, the colour of some clothing or a pair of shoes. There is old Edward, my lord's steward. What is he doing here? He should be at home, preparing for the harvest or sitting, watching his grandchildren play. Why did he come? To serve his lord, of course. It was his duty. But who is left to harvest the crops now?

I move on, the bodies thick on the ground now, the wounds greater. He must be here, in the heart of the battle dead. Ah, there is Wulfmaer, cheeks rosy in the dying light, but beneath the lying glow, cold and bloodless. His eyes stare into mine, surprised in death. I close them and remember. He was son to my lord's sister, brought up by him, who had no sons to call his own. So many men's sons came to him, when he was great in fame, to be trained in weapons, to learn to become great men, but none as great as him.

Close by is Aelfwine, another kinsman of my lord. I knew his father, his grandfather as well. His uncle was an Ealdorman of Mercia for many years. Young Aelfwine will never attain such high rank now.

A flash of colour holds my eye. This was my lord's banner, sewn by his wife. She will mourn his loss, perhaps. She has long wanted to embroider a cloth to celebrate his great deeds. A modest man, he always forbade it. Now she will have her way. Perhaps she will hang it in the Abbey above his grave, for men to remember him for ever more. I smooth the cool silk. I need no reminder.

He must be somewhere near. I search the gloom. The light is fading. There! A hand. I crawl closer. Yes, that is his. Long fingers relaxed that should be clasped around his sword's hilt. I trace the scars that map the surface. Some old wounds, barely visible, others new, red raw, unhealed.

It is hard to see now. Either the fall of night or tears dim my eyes, I know not which. I run my hand up the arm. It is starting to grow stiff. I must straighten it before the immobility of death falls upon his body. A wound near separates limb from body, nothing else would have forced him to drop his sword. This is what caused his death. Without his golden hilted sword, he could not fight, and so he died. What other wounds will I find upon his body?

I reach the shoulder, still broad and strongly muscled, even after all these years. He may have been a venerable adviser to the king, but he never let himself grow soft. I hesitate. Something is not right. I stretch my hand to touch his face and encounter… nothing. I hold my breath and feel the blood, still sticky, that covers the knob of bone that is all that remains. Was he dead when it happened or did that noble blood spurt like a fountain to mark his murderers?

Once he stood tall, towering above others. Now he is diminished, reduced to the stature of an ordinary man. The enemy knew his worth. They have taken the head of this famous warrior, to prove their own prowess in battle. Thieves steal honour that they cannot achieve themselves.

I arrange the body. Straighten the long legs and place his arms at his side. I tumble other bodies out of the way. I would know who they are, but I do not care, they are mere lumps of meat, I feel around the blood-sodden ground for his sword. It is not there. Did one of his companions scoop it up to continue the fight, or was that taken as well by the invaders?

It is quiet now. I hear the distant sound of celebration from the town. Why do they celebrate when my lord is dead? Because they are safe; safe to eat and drink, then go to their beds without fear. While he lies here, on the old ground, his duty done. They think the raiders have gone forever. They have not. They will be back, but who will defend this land then? The councillors who advise the king say that our land is rich. We can afford to pay them to go away. It will fail. They will always come back, greedy for our gold. Then, when we have no more to give them, they will come and take our land as well, and make us slaves.

A mournful note echoes across the field of dead. A pale shape floats on silent wings. Another soul ascending to heaven? Or just an owl hunting for a meal? Other animals will be searching for food. I must remain and defend his body until the day returns. It will not be hard; the nights are short this time of year. I will sit here beside him and pray for his soul. And remember. So much to remember.

Days were warmer and winters colder then, and the sun always shone. We would ride all day, racing on the hills or hunting in the forest. Our horses were strong, and our dogs were swift. I remember hunting wolves in the north. He still possessed the skin of one. Whose body will it warm now? I remember fishing in the rivers, the fish were shinier and their flesh more tender than those I find on my plate nowadays.

At night we would eat and drink. Many times the

mead horn would circulate, and we would drink deep of it. We would listen to the scop*, telling tales of heroes long ago. Later we would boast of our own deeds; our battles always ended in victory. Then there were the women… but monks are not supposed to think of that.

Life was so much simpler. A man knew what he should do and did it. Not like now, when everything is politics, and rich men strive for more riches, even the churchmen. Especially the churchmen. Have times changed or is it that we have grown old?

They say the world will end soon; a thousand years after the birth of Our Saviour. I will see my friend again, if not before. I do not think I will long outlive him. But I still have work to do.

Does the sky brighten? Nearby, the dark, treacherous river laps against a muddy shore. Is the bridge covered now, or open to the island? Yesterday it was important, but now it no longer matters. A gentle breeze stirs the battle stink. Somewhere a bird begins to sing. Soon the cart will come. I stretch my legs, stiff from the night watch.

I find the piece of silk, and before it is light enough to see the damage, I place it over the area of his missing head. Despite the desecration, I am glad I do not have to look into his dead eyes. That I could not have borne. I puzzle at the white feathers that move in the wind. No, not feathers; wisps of hair, white as swan's down. Shorn from his beard when his head was roughly hacked off. I carefully collect them and save them between the pages of my prayer book. I will place them in the coffin, most of them. Perhaps one small curl I will keep, for remembrance.

People return, some with pallets or carts to carry away their friends. Others bring spades to bury the unknown dead. Soon the grass will grow again, thicker than before, fed by the blood spilt here. Eventually, they will forget that anything important ever happened, in this field beside the cold dark Panta river.

It must not be forgotten. That will be my final work.

We will take his broken body to Ely. I will wash it and anoint it with precious oils. I will wrap it with costly cloths and place it in the coffin. A ball of scented beeswax, studded with his hair, to replace his head.

Then, when all is over.

When I have spoken to those few men that survived or witnessed from afar.

Then I will select the palest, smoothest parchment. I will grind the finest colours to make the ink. I will find the best of geese, select the straightest of their feathers and cut them to the perfect point.

Then I will write. I will tell the story of this battle on the field near Maldon. I will tell of the words they spoke and the weapons they used.

And I will tell of the death of the great Lord Byrhtnoth, son of Byrhthelm, Ealdorman of Essex, leader of the army of Aethelraed, King of England.

My friend.

*Scop - The anglo-saxon equivalent of a bard or minstrel. The person who would entertain the feasters in the lord's mead hall with poetry, music and the telling of tales.

Christine Hancock

Lover

Your body against mine was strong.
Your eyes were bright and full of life.

As I think of you, I remember your brow.
It showed character, and a need to be free.
Your weather worn face, like a cliff's edge,
Softened by the lapping waves of the sea.

Red hair, falling on masculine shoulders.
Broken veins camouflaged by freckles,
But the age spots were apparent to me.

The loosening skin on your wrists,
A contrast to your muscular arms.
How it felt when your sinews tightened,
With each breath, I'd submit to your charms.

I remember so clearly your powerful legs,
how they flinched
when I ran my fingers down your spine.
The rise and fall of your buttocks -
and for the next little while, you were mine.

When your loving was strong, every muscle taut.
When your breathing grew loud,
Our shared happiness, intense.

I can only think of you now,
as you were then, not as you are.

Madalyn Morgan

A Train Journey to Bentley

Caught the 9.33 delayed train, going to Bentley, near
Farnham
Bound for Milton Keynes, delayed by seven minutes,
Due to reported cow on the line. Poor thing
No problem for me. Time for the next of three trains.
   Ratley, tatley, rattle

Now due to travel to Clapham Junction
Oh no, children joined my train carriage
Charlie, about three years and Johnny maybe six
Seemingly their first exciting train journey
   Ratley, tatley, rattle

'There's a cow', one said, 'Look, a horse'
Piped in the second boy. 'I saw it first'
'No you didn't. Mummy, I saw it first, didn't I?'
Diplomatic Mummy's voice replied, 'It was together.'
   Ratley, tatley, rattle

'I want the blue pencil,' said one, loudly
'You both have blue pencils,' said Mummy
'I want to sit with Mummy, can I?'
'You are alright where you are, sit still.'
   Ratley, tatley, rattle

West Brompton the next stop, they're off,
They got off the train, all will be quiet - now.
Relax, travelling fast, next stop Clapham
Seats comfortable, seats to spare.
   Ratley, tatley, rattle.

There was time for prepared lunch. Thanks to
Peter, husband, kindly made cheese and tomato,
Two rolls, tasty, tomato soaked bread, yum.
Seedy rolls, good, finished lunch. We've arrived.
No more
        Ratley, tatley, rattle.

Kate A. Harris

My Father the Artist

Your fingers were tapered, knuckles knobbly,
they were messengers
carrying oil paint from your soul to your hands
and the shiver that ran through your shoulders
as the creative urge seized you. As a child
I used to wait and watch by your side,
brushes, turpentine,
record-player thundering Mahler or Beethoven
while your blank canvas sat on the easel
taunting you with its hunger for colour
begging to be fed with life

Images hiding in the dark recesses of your history
stayed like you, prisoners-of-war
Though that cruelty was decades distant
you couldn't paint the pain away,
you had your way to deal with it
let memories like seeds
lie dormant perhaps forever
underneath that higher joyous plain
of warm home-comings, a loving wife,
our family life, companionship and peace

And all the other things were left unsaid
potato peelings, mouldy bread
the blank canvas speaks and you,
as though in prayer,
give devoted concentration of intense imagination
to create form, structure, vision
You splash bright colours, fresh as fruit split open

wet with juice, ochre, cobalt, vermillion,
strewn across the canvas, generous and free

If half your energy was mine, I'd never wilt
but rather write and paint and work
until my breath was done
For you, it was impossible to stem that flow of lifeblood
Art to you was everything as you were, still are,
forever inspirational to me, my dearest father

Theresa Le Flem

Snow

White fluffy flecks fell silently from the sky, drawing heaven closer to earth in ever increasing luminous spirals, sucking the ground inwards and upwards. By morning, thick fluffed-up pillows covered every surface, like candy-floss piped from God's very own funfair machine. No surface had escaped, not a single fence panel, window sill, leaf or stone. The paddock itself seemed to have shrunk, its ground level raised by the thick inflated blanket. Shrieks of excitement trumpeted through the house, followed by muffled thuds of desperate pushing and shoving at the door, and then, finally breaking out of the barricaded house, we piled out, voices muted by the harsh cold meeting our open mouths.

The virgin snow lay thick and inviting beyond the gate opening into the paddock, nature's very own playground. A newly plumped-up alabaster duvet lay in front of us, dulled only by the grey of a sky threatening yet further downfall, beckoning us to leap onto it, but forbidding us in equal measure. Hesitation succumbed to impulse as we launched ourselves onto the cushioned ground, obliterating the dainty lacework created by the birds that had beaten us to it. We threw ourselves around like feral animals, hearts thumping, eyes stinging. The prehistoric grunts emanating from our flailing bodies transformed themselves into whoops of devilish delight. Like atoms reorganising themselves after the big bang, our desires became manifest. Snow tennis balls grew into footballs and then giant lead-filled beach balls as we rolled them along with a crunch, initially chasing them and then finally heaving them with the whole force of our padded bodies. Rolls of snowy turf arranged themselves into a circle with a gap for an entrance. Layer upon layer, the shell of our construction grew upwards and inwards into the dome of an Inuit cathedral. We toiled like ants carrying multiple times their body weight under the force of social compulsion to get the job done, albeit with much heaving, puffing, grunting and sweating. After considerable scraping, smoothing and filling in, we stood back and marvelled at our creation.

Huddled in the belly of our frozen womb, our eyes chased the vaporised puffs of breath that emerged rhythmically from our puckered mouths while we bathed in our collaborative sense of accomplishment, as if in worship to an Arctic god. Suddenly, metallic mugs of steaming hot chocolate were handed through the gateway of our new temple, and ceremoniously passed from one child to the next like silver chalices. Hot liquid cautiously passed our lips and the warm nectar seeped into our bloodstreams. Digestive biscuits, broken in half and dunked, merged with our flesh. As one with each other and our own creator, we communed in silence. One breath, one body, one being. Our radiating souls warmed the inner walls of our sanctuary causing glistening, transparent jewels to drip randomly onto our bobble hat crowns. Unspoken grief began to creep slowly into our hearts as we subconsciously accepted the reality of our impending loss. We had gained, we had conquered and we had constructed, but we knew that the fall was inevitable. As the sun weakened in the sky, and the mugs of cocoa ran dry, we knew that the time had come to say 'Adieu'. Instinctively, like Egyptian kings, we each left an eternal object at the altar of our childhood: a stick, a stone, a broken eraser dug up from deep within a coat pocket.

One by one, we tentatively crawled through the tiny tunnel we had carved out, squeezing our puffed up bodies through the icy birth canal, only to be struck by the chilling harshness of the dusky air in our faces. With heavy legs and hearts, all bursting with growing pains, we stood and contemplated our rebirth. Then, turning our backs, somehow knowing that we would never again return to this moment, we trudged home to the bricks and mortar of our other worlds.

Sandrine Pickering

What's all the Fuss About?

She looked around: there was really nothing more to be done here. She picked up her bag and left.

She too had been fifteen, all those years ago, and had been lucky to find a refuge from the awfulness of it all. Well, she thought she was safe until Father O'Flaherty had given her one of those looks that she recognised from home. Back there it was always mixed up with her father's drunkenness but, as she had grown more artful, she usually managed to keep him at bay until he became incapable. He would be sober in the morning and then it was as if nothing had happened. Her mother had no idea of what went on, or rather, as she came to realise later, chose not to notice.

Father O'Flaherty didn't get drunk like her Da, not in the church anyway. He would compliment her on the flowers and admire the gleaming brass work of the pulpit. He even attended choir practice, despite having a voice like a raven, and for a while she persuaded herself it was her friend Eileish he was after, and so he may have been, but it wasn't the sort of thing to discuss about a priest, even with Eileish. Matters had come to a head when her Da was off work, sick: well, Ma said that was it but he got a lot better in the middle of the day and the Church seemed the safer option.

On her hands and knees, scrubbing the vestry floor, she didn't hear anything until the door clicked shut. Afterwards she found herself sharing a secret 'To the Glory of God' according to Father O'Flaherty but 'just between the two of them' he'd said. She had to agree with him on one point, no one else would understand, or believe, so she had kept the secret as long as she could.

But there was no way she could keep it from Da if she stayed at home. In the end he'd notice and if she went into one of those terrible homes for girls in her condition, even miles away, one of his mates would find out and tell him. Policemen and Priests were the same; they kept tabs on that sort of thing.

She went to London and stayed with her elder sister. Theresa's man had gone there for the work years ago and they'd set up home together. As a small child she'd assumed Theresa was married, that's what grown-ups did before they had children she'd thought, and there were several of them around now, but no sign of a man. One little boy had a very dark skin. She didn't ask: but she did confide in Theresa about her condition.

'I was waiting for y' to tell me,' her sister said. How on earth did Theresa know she wondered?

'Who was it, Da, the Priest, a fella? No... don't say, 'tis easier not knowing. If y' don't tell me y' don't have to tell y'self.'

When she had first arrived she'd seen the empty stout bottles in the backyard and had thought Theresa's husband must have been a drunkard like their father but that evening she realised her mistake.

'Come on lassie, it might do the job for y'.' There was none of the shiny glass with its rich dark liquid and creamy foaming head. If the stout was going to do anything for her it would have to do it straight from the bottle. She wasn't keeping up with her older sister, and after two bottles she was sick.

'What a waste of Guinness; that lot wasn't 'Good for You' at all, now was it?' Theresa giggled, 'and it won't do the business neither.'

121

She discovered later what was expected of a slug of alcohol in an unwanted pregnancy, but back then Theresa's attempt to help just slid into the grey morass of things she didn't know, or more often, didn't want to know. Young Liam for a start, sharing a mattress on the floor, whilst she occupied the bed, with his three brothers, their white faces so different from his dark one. The issue remained dormant until Theresa insisted she got a job.

'Can't keep you wid out some money coming in,' she said. 'It costs to feed y'.' Up till then she'd thought the child minding was sufficient recompense for bed and board. Theresa's work seemed to occupy most evenings, even nights, certainly everyone else was in bed by the time she came home. It was another item for the grey morass when it became plain that Theresa was out at night whether or not there was a younger sister to take care of the children.

It was easy work, washing dishes in a café, for a girl who'd scrubbed and polished at St Michael's. Through the door that divided café from kitchen there were occasional glimpses of the clientele. Back home every face was white, or like Father O'Flaherty, florid with excess: but sitting at the tables, drinking cups of stewed tea and eating stale sandwiches were black faces, joking and laughing. She wasn't sure whether this was a reality she needed to hide from or not. Dressed in their colourful clothes, they seemed to enjoy the craic as much as the Irish, not that she understood their Caribbean patois any more than they understood her brogue on the odd occasion when she was set on to clear tables.

Between home and work was another surprise. The evening she first arrived, after a confusing bus ride in the dark, from the station, she'd walked past an intimidating black void before she found where her sister lived. Back home with the countryside so close, no one had ever thought the town needed a green space, but later, in the daylight, she saw that Grange Park was full of noisy children on the grass, their harassed mums, and more sedate citizens, taking the air on a path round its perimeter. As she got nearer her time she would flop, gratefully, onto one of the park benches, on her way home from work. Too late she realised she was sharing her seat with one of them. Worse still the man smiled as he caught her eye.

'See you in the café, don't I?'

Holy Mother of God she thought, he wants to talk as well. It was only as she was struggling to her feet that she recognised the elderly West Indian as a customer who had given her his chair when she'd had that funny turn.

'You alright now Missee?' There was concern in his eyes. 'You a bit unsteady t'other day.' She smiled her reply as she sank back onto the bench.

In the end she had to give in her notice, the sink was just too far away, beyond her swollen belly, to manage the washing up. With a heavy heart she found herself telling her friend in the park why she wouldn't be coming there any more.

'You come by an' tell me how you get on and mebbe bring baby when it arrive.' Neither knew the other's name, despite weeks of regular meetings.

'Of course, when it's all over,' she said. Was that a lie she wondered, something else to slip into the morass of things to forget. She burst into tears, and found the old man's comforting arm round her shoulder.

Their moments together had been the only gleam

of light in the dark awfulness of her life since... since it happened.

They had talked, often enough only half understanding each other, of their lives back home and of the confusing things they had found in London. Rooms to let with those horrible signs, No Blacks, No Irish, No Dogs had drawn them together even as they were both appalled at the inhumanity of it. In her more fanciful moments she pitied the dogs. The two of them at least had each other.

*

The pains, when they came, were bad enough to start with, but once the baby was coming it was agonizing: she felt she was being torn apart from the inside. Theresa had lied. She'd said, 'it was easy as shelling peas.' If the girl had been able, she would have stopped things there and then, but like the rest of her life, she had no control, only this time it was different, and between the contractions there was some satisfaction in the inevitability of it all.

She screamed when the pain got too bad. 'Will yer stop all that noise. You girls have yer fun an' yer have t' pay for it.' The midwife, when she arrived, had sent all the children packing. Theresa had boiled some water as requested but then she too had disappeared. The only target for the woman's disapproval was the labouring girl.

Throughout her pregnancy she had not thought of the child that shared her body as a life. The trouble the baby had brought her and Theresa, yes; the shame of bearing a bastard, yes; and just now the pain she'd had to endure at the birth, yes; but the baby as a person had

GET TO THE POINT

been blanked out.

Now, when it was all over, with the little pink blob of life cradled in her arms, and despite the soreness and exhaustion, a great wave of tenderness engulfed everything. She felt for the baby boy as she'd never felt for anyone in her life before.

'The adoption lady says she can't come for a day or two, so you'll have t'manage till then.' For the moment, in the rush of emotion, the midwife's message didn't register, nor did her instruction to 'Give the bab a bottle, it'll be easier that way.'

Earlier when she'd been with her sister to see the agency, she'd been silent. Somehow there weren't any answers to their questions. Theresa had done the talking and the whole thing dissolved into a blur so there was very little to recollect afterwards. It was a shock when finally the adoption lady did come and what arrived with her was pain, pain that was worse than the pangs of giving birth.

Little Aidan was feeding whilst the woman stood there in her dark suit and gabardine patting a briefcase.

'Come along now, I haven't got all day. You know it's for the best.' She took the baby straight from his mother's breast. 'Anyway, you signed these papers.'

Afterwards the pain seemed unendurable. In the end it evolved into an impenetrable blanket of despair. The pain had penetrated from the outside but the depression came from within. It destroyed the girl's will and she took to her bed.

'You'll not improve until y'r back home,' was Theresa's view. 'Anyways, I've got another on the way now and we haven't got the room.'

So it was that the grieving mother was led to Euston station and cajoled into a third class seat on the

Boat Train. 'She's not herself,' Theresa told the guard. 'When y' get to Holyhead, could y' just see she gets onto the Dun Laoghaire ferry.'

The girl had no plan and had no will to implement one anyway. She was crouching, huddled in a corner of the quay, shivering and staring hopelessly across the inviting waters of the harbour when the Walking Nuns found her and took her away.

'At least we got her before she jumped.' The two of them talked over the girl. One each side, they marched her purposefully toward a bus stop.

'We don't know what she's called?' said the other.

'We could try asking her I suppose.'

The girl didn't have a name, not that she could remember anyway. Later as she lay on a cold hard bed, in her empty misery, the waters of Dun Laoghaire harbour beckoned to her again that night, and for many after.

The Sisters of Mercy gave her a name, Assumpta, and this priceless gift enabled the girl to take the first faltering steps toward rebuilding herself. It took many months during which she was given much else besides a name, but the succour came with a price: the Sisters made her one of their own.

*

Sister Assumpta has done her best for them over the years and just now she is working for the Glory of God with another fifteen-year-old girl.

'Do be quiet child, 'tis for the best.'

The girl continues to wail.

'You know y'll never be allowed t' keep the bab, and he'll be much better off wid someone who can look after him proper.'

The young mother won't be pacified; she's screaming abuse now.

'Well, all I can say is, you've had y're fun,' Sister Assumpta packs her things away, 'and now tis only right y' pay for it.'

She looks around, with the child in the crook of one arm: there's really nothing more to be done here. She picks up her bag and leaves.

David J. Boulton

Garden

For Jen, Beric, Alaric and Sorrel

You are my garden
Seeds that I nurtured
Seedlings I protected
From the heat, from the cold
From harm

You are my garden
Shooting up tall in your Springtime
Flowering in your Summer
Each blossom bright, and strong

Growing in different ways to fulfilment
Wonderful to watch
Filling me with happiness
More than I deserve

Maturing now, my garden
Autumn is round the corner
But I will not see it
For it's Winter where I am

You are my garden
My peace, my haven
My joy

E. E. Blythe

Christmas Switch-on

Tonight the town's awash with brain-
bashing din, as well as rain.
The mayor and corp are in the square
with all the young and younger there
to watch the switching-on of lights
to brighten up pre-Christmas nights.
The lights, alas, are much the same
as last year's, but they all came
to spend their cash on roll-a-penny,
and fairground rides, of which there's many.
Instead of a penny it's now a pound
to ride upon the merry-go-round.

Carousels with organs roaring,
(with luck they'll stop before the morning);
bumper cars with crackles and bashes,
yells and screams, and sometimes gashes;
dive-bombers with young girls squealing
all together now, with feeling;
bouncy castles with children squeaking.
We just can't hear ourselves speaking
in our monthly writers' meeting,
above the unrelenting beating,
while just outside the ghost train wheezes,
howls and moans whenever it pleases.

The roads within the town have bars
with long diversions for all cars
and parking spots are madly sought,
for love or money can't be bought,

so add to all this noise and bustle
hoots and shrieking brakes and hustle.
And over all there's such a racket
as fairground people make a packet,
with heaven-rending, ear-drum splitting
so-called music, hardly fitting
small-town Sunday evening streets.
And still the throbbing music beats
and echoes round the empty shops
until, with one last bang it stops.

Wendy Goulstone

Autumn

All is briskly cold
the wind it has a bite.
Where once was dew at early morn
Is clothed with frosty white.

The leaves are falling down
to hide the dormant soil
the squirrel gathers nuts for food
no time to cease his toil

Cobwebs strung on gorse
spangled dripping wet
The badger will not venture out
he slumbers in his sett

The dormouse weary now
into her nest will crawl
soon now the snow will come
like silent sleep will fall.

Ruth Hughes

Didn't They Know?

She walked the streets not knowing what to do or where to go. The sun blazed, bouncing heat and dazzling sparkles of light into her eyes. Why was everything so bright?

Flowers spread their colourful, scented glory wherever they got a purchase, swaying gently in the breeze. Why was everything so peaceful?

Birds sang and played in the rainbow of spray feeding a sodden lawn. Why was everything so happy?

Didn't they know? Didn't they know?

She carried on walking.

A dog barked madly at her through a living room window making her jump at the crack in the stillness. She stopped and stared. It was a young animal but its fur was matted and dark and it bounced all over, scratching at the glass, leaving bloody smears, desperate to escape its confines.

Her feet took her to the house and the dog went frantic. It was out the door and down the street before she even realised she had opened it. She didn't go in, she knew better than that now.

She carried on walking.

The stillness had weight. It lay over her shoulders like a thick shroud. In her head was nothing but a sound like the hiss and crackle of a record stuck on 'didn't they know?' She carried on walking.

At first she thought the ringing was just in her head but it penetrated the fog of her mind and she woke suddenly as from a dream blinking and bewildered. She chased the sound, hope bellowing in her chest.

The door was red, the paint was chipped but the

lock was open and she burst into the hallway and fell onto the phone like a starving person onto a banquet.

'Hello?' Her voice cracked into the receiver – when was the last time she had spoken out loud? A few days? A week? 'Hello?', she tried again, her voice stronger – hope, a tangible thing, alive and wriggling.

At first she didn't understand, just relishing the sound of another human being, but then realisation dawned and hope drowned. How she had hated these automated sales calls, how she had wished they would stop pestering her at all times of the day – now she couldn't bear to drop the receiver but the smell was beginning to register with her and she could feel the 'openness' of the door behind her into what she could only assume would be the kitchen. She didn't want to see in there. She had seen all of that the first few days and knew now it would be worse. She left.

She carried on walking.

She supposed she should feel grateful. The thing had happened early in the morning, most people still in their beds. The few who had fallen in the streets had long since been stripped and dragged off by scavengers. She didn't have to deal with piles of the dead.

At first, she had believed she would find survivors, she had survived after all. The wave of death that had swept over what she could only assume was the whole world had missed her, surely it had missed others. But the television stations were dead, the radio was just static, there were no distant noises of people, nothing. Just her, the animals and the stillness.

She walked the streets not knowing what to do or where to go.

Terri Brown

Unexpected Destiny

Being careful not to trip up in my shiny stilettos, I carried the tray of hot drinks from the kitchen and passed them out to my colleagues. I always volunteered to make the drinks whenever I could. It was the perfect escape from the humdrum of data entry.

'Vanessa Stapleton? Vanessa Stapleton!' A male voice was suddenly hollering my name across our large open plan office. 'Vanessa Stapleton!'

He came into view. He was tall and skinny and wearing a perfectly tailored suit. He had everyone's attention, but it was far too weird for anyone to react.

'Vanessa Stapleton!'

'Here,' I murmured, highly embarrassed. I stood up from my desk to meet his piercing blue eyes.

'At last!' he said approaching me. He was eloquent and graceful, although he had a fiery dominance about him. 'You must be so excited. Your time has come.'

The only thing I could conclude was that I was being somehow surprised by one of those TV shows. It was the sort of thing my boyfriend would set me up for. I expected cameras to appear any second, and perhaps a celebrity. But other than this man's eyes burning a hole into my soul, nothing happened at all.

I glanced across the dozens of faces around me. My peers seemed fascinated by the drama that was playing out in front of them.

'Shall we go outside?' I said to the man, locking my computer and grabbing my bag. 'I'll have an early lunch,' I said to my team around me.

'Wonderful,' the strange man said, grinning from

ear to ear.

I led the way out of the office, deliberately looking to the floor to avoid the open-mouthed stares of my colleagues. I hated being a spectacle.

'Who are you?' I asked as we stepped in the lift, still expecting a celebrity or two to leap out at me.

'I'm your destiny, of course,' he said, and it made my skin crawl. He wasn't unattractive, but he was a bit pompous, and definitely a weirdo.

'I have a boyfriend,' I said, defensively.

'No harm's going to come to him,' he said, as if that was a perfectly reasonable response.

'Is any harm going to come to me?' I muttered. I was now trembling. What was I doing leaving the office with this man? Was I walking into my own demise? Was this the end of the road for me and I was happily playing along?

He guffawed loudly. 'Embrace it, darling. You've waited a lifetime for this. It's exciting.'

We reached the lobby. I told myself I should be running far away from this peculiar man, but an inexplicable compulsion was making me stay very much by his side.

'Shall we grab a coffee?' I said. I might not have felt the urge to leave, but at least I could make sure we stayed around witnesses.

He addressed me with confusion. 'Why are you delaying things? Let's get on with it. I have places to be.'

'Get on with what?' I asked, horrified.

'Where's your bracelet?' he asked, searching my bare arms.

'I haven't got a bracelet.'

'You must wear it at all times.'

'I haven't got a bracelet. I've never worn a

bracelet. I think you've got the wrong woman. Can I go back to my desk now?'

'You are Vanessa Stapleton? Yes, I can feel your aura. But why aren't you wearing your bracelet?'

I didn't know what to say. He was obviously a nutter.

More fascinated eyes became drawn in our direction. He was so animated as he spoke.

'There's a park outside,' I said. I needed to get away from people I knew. 'Shall we go and talk there? Enjoy a bit of the sun?'

'See, you're attracted to the heat. It's obviously you.'

I nodded as if I knew exactly what he was wittering on about, and I led us out of the safety of my office building, across the busy road, and into the small park opposite. I sat on the first bench I could find, making sure that the ten-storey building I'd just been in was still very much in view.

'You seem confused,' he said, sitting down next to me. 'I normally get either rapturous delight at my appearance or absolute fear. I've had many a man bawling at my feet, begging for it to not be their turn; obviously not understanding the honour that has been bestowed upon them. I'm prepared for that. I'm certainly not prepared for your utter confusion. Is this a trick?'

I started to mumble a few words, but nothing of any sense came out. I paused and took a few deep breaths. 'Is this a set up?' I finally asked.

'What have you done with your bracelet?' he asked. 'When your parents gave it to you, what did you do with it?'

I shook my head. 'I've never had a bracelet from

my parents. I promise.'

'But surely they must have told you about your destiny? Did you not ask where your bracelet was?'

'I don't know what you're talking about.'

'Your destiny. What did your parents tell you about your destiny?'

I shrugged. 'They just wanted me to be happy.'

He paused and became deadly serious for the first time. 'Are you telling me that you genuinely don't know who I am or why I'm here?'

'Yes,' I nodded.

He sighed and stood up. He started tutting and pacing around. 'Your parents have been very naughty. Very naughty indeed. Are you sure you're not just really clever and you're avoiding reaching your destiny?'

I shook my head as he studied me.

'No,' he said. 'I can see the ignorance in your eyes. You're completely lost.'

I wanted to be offended, but I was actually more relieved.

'Your parents are going to suffer for this.'

'My parents died,' I replied. 'They died three years ago.'

'I know,' he said, like I was an idiot. 'But they're not getting out of it that easily.'

Yep, he was definitely a nutter.

'I suppose we could track down your bracelet,' he said. 'They probably sold it. It is three thousand years old. Probably worth a bit.' He shook his head as if to disagree with himself before he exhaled sharply. 'They're going to have to face the consequences of their frivolous actions. That's for sure.'

'Can I go now?' I asked.

'No, we need to figure this out. You're needed for a

job. What am I supposed to tell the boss? He's making cuts all over the place. I don't want to have to do it. It's your bloody destiny.'

I didn't know what to say. I stared back at my office, checking it was still there.

He sighed with frustration again. 'But you're an adult now, aren't you?'

'Yes,' I nodded. 'I'm twenty-four.'

'You're not going to have time. You're supposed to bond with your bracelet during your formative years. I mean the power's in you, not your bracelet, but without it how are you supposed to control it? Oh, this could get very messy. This is far beyond my pay grade.'

'What?' I was now becoming quite concerned.

'I think we'll have to end things here, don't you? I think it's too late. Such a shame. He'll go mad, of course, but it's not my fault. Serves him right for cutting back. I'll be off then. I'm really sorry I haven't been able to give you your assignment. It was a juicy one as well. Most first timers don't get such pleasure. You would have loved it.'

'You're going?' I asked, totally bewildered.

'I'll have to.' He went to turn away from me when he snapped back. 'Just don't worry if lightning comes out of your fingers, or you start glowing red. Oh, I hope you're not one of those who turn to metal. That's painful. I'll guess we'll just have to wait and see. I'll try to get a caseworker out to see you. But again, you know, these cutbacks. Just hang on in there. And if it does get bad, blame your parents.'

'What are you talking about?'

'Too-da-loo, then. Best of luck!' With that he instantly vanished. Vanished into thin air. Gone without so much as even a puff of smoke.

I stared around, hoping for something to make sense.

Maybe now the cameras were going to appear. Maybe it was time for the celebrity to pop out of the trees.

I sat there for a short while, but the only thing to change was my increased nausea over how sinister that whole experience had been.

I grabbed a sandwich from the bakery nearby and I headed back to the office. The last thing I felt like was working again. My head was all over the place.

'Who was that?' my friend asked as I sat back at my desk.

'I have no idea. I think he knew my parents.'

'He was a bit creepy. How did he even get in the building?'

My skin prickled as her question sank in. We were in very secure premises. You needed a pass to get in, or reception would call if you had a visitor. He'd just appeared on our floor. I didn't think that was even possible.

'I have no idea,' I replied. 'The whole thing was really odd.'

'Never mind. My parents have got some strange friends, too.'

'Yeah.'

I tapped on my keyboard to unlock my computer and I opened up Google. I was still on my lunch, technically, so I decided to check the sales. I needed a bit of retail therapy after such a shock.

As I grabbed my mouse, a small red glow caught the corner of my eye. I looked down to see my fingers flaming.

'What the!'

'Are you okay?' my friend said.

I studied my fingers again. They were back to normal, although the faint whiff of burning hovered in the air.

'Yeah,' I said, feeling anything but okay.

I watched my hands, but nothing else happened.

Nothing happened for the rest of the day.

But I got the feeling that my life was never going to be quite the same again.

Lindsay Woodward

Jimmy, Packing To Go On Holiday

'I knew before she started packing,
Mum wouldn't let me take my skates.
So while she wasn't looking,
I put them in Dad's case.

'You're not taking a kite,' she said,
As I flew it through the door.
Spiderman, above my head.
'I've told you, nothing more!'

'Oh, Mum!' I said, 'it's very small.
It can go right in your case.'
Mum looked at me and rolled her eyes.
'Leave me a little space.'

So the skates were packed, my cars, my kite.
My cricket bat and ball.
My X-Box, Drone, and Finger Spins,
But no underpants at all.

Madalyn Morgan

A Bat in the House

A flapping thing! An errant bat!
Inadvertently it's come indoors
out of the dark night, skimming and spinning
It takes the surfaces skilfully
missing everything in the room
but wildly round and round it flies, not stopping
Black as a piece of plastic sack

Make it stop!
It won't, it can't, can't catch it, slow it,
open the window latch!
It whizzes past unseeing
Blindly flying, flapping, crying
like a mad thing, silently
Get the switch! Turn off the light!

Suddenly the hush of the dark night beckons
the darkness outside creeps right in
through the open window, breathing …

The bat dives for freedom, fails!
Clings with its tiny baby fingers
to the curtain cloth,
It pants, it waits, watching,
eyes like jewels of jet, rolling
The skin of its wings stretched taut, waiting
Its crazy catlike whiskers twitch
It flicks and fumbles as I dive,
It's caught! It scrambles to escape!
I lift the drape, the panting bat affixed

and to the open window space
I offer it

A rush, a flash! The curtain slackens in my hand
A violent chill goes through me
as the cold night air reclaims its own
and leaves me there, alone

The bat has gone
and in a way
I mourn

Theresa Le Flem

Copied but loved...

I live in the Midlands
And All I know of the sea
Are Seagulls
Haarking
Atop telegraph poles
Not
mine

Chris Wright

A Fair Price

Magda tied her message to the dove's leg and threw it high into the air. The small white bird circled her once and flew out to sea towards the setting sun. Standing alone at the edge of the cliff, she watched it until it was nothing more than a small dot in the coral-streaked sky.

'My heart longs for you,' she whispered. 'My soul aches for you.'

A hand touched her shoulder. She turned and Daniel was there, his eyes reflecting her misery, his body reflecting her pain. She took his hand and they walked along the cliff path in silence until they reached the memorial to the lost children, a stone monolith with their names carved upon it.

Magda traced a name with her finger and then could bear it no longer. She sank to the ground, rocking back and forth, her body racked with grief.

'Not knowing, it's worse than death.'

Daniel held her close. 'It's the same for us all,' he said, his tears mingling with hers. He helped her to her feet and together they slowly made their way home through the fading twilight.

It was night by the time they reached the small fishing village. They walked down the narrow cobbled street, past the shuttered cottages and the dark, uninviting inn. There was no-one about. Strangers were no longer welcome and the villagers had nothing to be merry about.

In their cottage, Magda prepared a meal. She did not want to eat, but she knew if she did not, then Daniel would not eat either. So she ate and Daniel ate and the food tasted of nothing.

Early next morning Daniel and Magda went down to the quay where the fishing boats were waiting, eager to put to sea. More fish had been caught in the last year than ever before. Catches had doubled, trebled, quadrupled, yet there were few signs of the prosperity that such good fortune should bring. The fishermen saved their money to buy back the happiness they had sold to feed their greed.

*

Magda stood with the other women and watched in the pale morning light as the fishermen prepared to sail. She wondered if her message had been received, if it had been understood. Would he come? He'd promised he would return after a year and a day.

She heard a high-pitched sound, but it was a seagull crying in the wind. Again she heard a noise, but it was only a cat meowing. She picked it up and it purred in her arms. She looked at Daniel, but he shook his head and she put the cat down. It ran off between the waiting women and disappeared.

Then Magda heard another sound, the high, pure, sweet sound of pipes, like the sun sparkling on the water. She turned and there he was, standing in front of the boats, playing her pipes. He looked the same, dressed all in red and yellow, his straw-coloured hair hanging to his shoulders.

Magda couldn't speak, only point. Daniel was by her side, holding her back as she tried to move. The people watched in silence as the piper walked towards them, still playing his sweet music.

He stopped a few feet away and said, 'Has it been a

146

good year? Have you prospered?'

Daniel stepped forward. 'You know that we have. The fish leap into our nets wherever we cast them. We have become rich, but we have not spent our wealth. It is all yours. Everything we have is yours.'

He laid his full purse at the piper's feet. The rest of the villagers laid their money down one by one.

'Take whatever you want. Return our children, we beg of you.'

The piper laughed. 'Now you offer money,' he said. 'Tell me, was our bargain worth it?'

He took up his pipes and played a slow, haunting melody of unbearable sadness that made the villagers feel their grief anew. Before they had time to weep, the music changed. It had a stern theme that scolded them like a strict parent and they hung their heads in shame. The pipes fell silent for a moment and then began a merry song, a happy song like the sounds of children laughing and playing.

It took a few moments for the people to realise that it was the sound of children, their children. They came running down the cobbled street, laughing and crying for joy as they saw their parents once more.

Magda saw Adam, her only child, among them. She ran to him and picked him up, holding him close to her heart, tears of joy upon her face. Mothers and fathers reclaimed their lost children, rejoicing and weeping from happiness. They hugged and kissed their sons and daughters.

The piper was picking up his money and stowing it about his person. Magda saw him and she handed Adam to Daniel. She walked towards the piper, terrible in her anger, yet ice-cold in her rage. The piper looked up to see her and he smiled, a knowing smile, a sly smile. A year of anguish and torment welled up inside her and she struck out blindly at him. Shaken by the unexpected blow, he slipped on the cobblestones and fell, spilling the coins.

For a moment no-one moved. Then as one all the mothers relinquished their children to their fathers and advanced on the piper. The men turned their children away, so they could not see as the women wreaked their vengeance in a silence that made it all the more terrible. When their thirst for retribution was quenched, there was nothing left of the piper but his pipes. Pieces of his scarlet and yellow garments fluttered in the sea breeze and the cobbles glistened red. All the while the men had ignored such a dreadful sight as they hugged and kissed their long lost sons and daughters.

Magda picked up the pipes and walked to the edge of the quay. She flung them high in the air and they tumbled over and over, gleaming in the sunlight, until they fell into the sea, disappearing beneath the waves.

Fran Neatherway

Fear of flying

The plane's wheels transferred the vibrations of the runway to Jack's seat but he was already trembling as he fought for breath. He let the air out, first from his lungs, then down below.

The quiet ones were more potent and if he could smell it the other passengers would too. But, not this time; nothing, not a whiff. Maybe he was so afraid, his brain had let go of smell to focus on fear. A man of sixty-three who was so afraid of flying he'd once soiled himself in a full cabin.

He felt the world tip on its axis as the plane lifted off. Then the change of gravity like your guts were being sucked out through your arse. The feeling he had when Bodine had got off the see-saw without warning and he crashed to the ground, winding himself and cracking his coccyx. Pain and nausea and Bodine laughing.

'Come along you two, time to bath. Beans for supper,' his mother sang out in her Irish brogue as though they didn't have beans every night but only on special days for a treat.

'Bodine, Jack, come inside.'

Bodine had hidden in the garden and left him in his agony and, when neither of them came, Mother fetched the wooden spoon.

'Jack Gledhill, you little devil, lying on the ground and playing dead when I call you. And you've chased Bodine again.

'I've told you before, she's only five and you're a full two years older and it's your job to play with her.'

He knew if she hit him with the spoon he would

die because his bum already hurt like there was a cactus up it.

But she sensed there was something wrong and tried to pick him up by the right armpit. He screamed as the broken bone moved in his lower back. Later, when he woke up he was lying on his tummy in the hospital with a pillow under his chest and his head hanging over it.

And sitting next to the bed was Father O'Leary.

There was a twinge in his coccyx now, and his spine; not unusual in a man of his age when take-off pulled you one way and gravity the other. Physio when he got home. That was nice. The two-hour deep-tissue massage. Expensive, but set him up for days.

He felt a movement in the bowels of the plane as the wheels tucked into their port and he drew hard with his lungs, but the air stuck in his throat.

'Try to breathe normally, Mr Gledhill,' said the air hostess and she placed a mask over his face. 'Breathe in and relax. I'll adjust the oxygen for you.'

Wow, airlines today. They had service down to such an art.

*

He felt better, but when he opened his eyes it was dark. Must be the mask, he thought.

The oxygen was cool and clean but it made him giddy. Maybe they put something in it to calm you down.

The seat was comfortable. First class. He had only ever flown first. Not quite true: his virgin flight when he was twenty-two had been economy from New York to DC. If it hadn't been so short, they would have landed mid-journey to let him off. Back then no one understood that fear of flying was a mental condition needing treatment.

'Just pull yourself together,' the first officer said when he was called and found Jack crying, wheezing and curled up like a foetus on the seat.

He was going to Washington for an interview and they had paid for the ticket. More than forty years ago. At least he got the job as a survey engineer, but from then on he travelled by road. When he specialised in building dams, he only took contracts where he could drive to the site - none of these fly-in larks.

He had flown transcontinental many times and long haul wasn't so bad because the doctor gave him pills. Go to sleep for eight or ten hours and that was it. Always first class where the chair was like a bed and he could sleep until just before landing.

Had he taken a pill this time? They made him so woozy, no surprise if he couldn't remember, but he must have.

Take off and landing were the worst and, if Margaret wasn't travelling, one of the crew would join him at the beginning and end of the flight. Just like today.

On trips where there wasn't time to sleep, Margaret would sit elsewhere. To cope with this thing, he had to be alone and his wife's incessant chatting drove him nuts. She couldn't help it. Said talking calmed her nerves. Didn't do much for his.

Right now, she was probably next to some passenger who wished they'd missed the flight.

This holiday to Africa was fine because the QEII took them from New York to Cape Town and they had a wonderful cruise. 'The Tavern of the Seas' was one of the most beautiful cities in the world, he thought. Table Mountain as the backdrop and the winding coastline creating dozens of hidden bays.

They took the ferry to Robben Island. Strange, but boats, regardless of how small and no matter how rough the sea, didn't even make him queasy, though Margaret had her head over the rails. Kept her quiet.

Nelson Mandela's jail cell was narrow and cold and no place to spend twenty-seven years. What a man.

Jack knew what it was like in jail. Two years - from the age of thirty - after the hit-and-run. Evidence was slim and he'd fought to reopen the case and clear his name, but life had to move on.

The thud was like the wheels of a plane docking after takeoff, a dull grunt that sounded in your gut and ricocheted through your lungs and into the jaw and only then to the ears. The boy didn't even scream.

He stopped with the only thought being to render help, but when he opened the kid's lips with his fingers to give him mouth-to-mouth there was vomit inside and it made Jack retch. Kid was motionless and there was nothing an ambulance could have done. Doctor was an arse to say in court that medics might have been able to save him. Two years for 'might'.

'Might!' His lawyer had played the word.

'My client "might" not have even been there that night.

'Records show an anonymous call was made to the police from a callbox and the police only arrived half-an-hour later! If they had been more efficient, they 'might' have found the boy still alive, or dead on impact.

'Either way, there's not enough evidence to find my client guilty.'

He was breathing more easily now and hadn't

brought up, just a sour taste in his throat. Is that what made him remember?

He'd fly to the moon if God would just let him go back to that night and do something for the boy walking home from school in the mist. To die with vomit in your mouth.

'Are you alright my son?' The voice was to his left, standing, talking down at him. 'God is always with us, even here.' Bloody priest on board. Last thing he needed.

Like Father O'Leary and his affair with Mrs Prendergast and even then, she with her good legs and low blouse wasn't enough. He had a good heart though and when anyone was in trouble, rich or poor, O'Leary would be there no matter the hour. Maybe it wasn't Mrs Prendergast, but who else could it be?

'Go away,' he said, but, through the mask his voice sounded like a vinyl record played at slow speed. 'Gorrywah.'

'You're a lying little shit, Jack Gledhill, just like your father when he comes home late from work. Lies, lies, lies!' and his mother smacked him on the shoulder each time she said the word.

He sat on the edge of his bed in silence.

'Father O'Leary would never do a thing like that. No priest would, not in the Catholic church. Never. And you'll be goin' to him for bible study as normal from next week and maybe he can teach you that lyin' is a sin,' and she stomped out of the room and slammed the door.

From Cape Town they had taken a luxury train up to Johannesburg and across the border into Botswana and north to Zambia and Victoria Falls.

What a sight. The world's largest falling curtain of

water. A mile wide and twice the height of Niagara. The water tumbled with such force, it sent a cloud of mist two miles into the sky, and a permanent rainbow hung over the gorge.

He and Margaret had made love at the hotel near Table Mountain. On the train too from Cape Town through Botswana to Bulawayo and on to Livingstone in Zambia. The cruise had softened the hurt of the affair and they were starting to find the breeze that had once blown between them.

He'd gone to jail only three years after their wedding and, although she still defended his innocence, she knew. Worse still, she knew he knew and it was an unwritten ransom note between them.

Not that he cared any more. It would be a relief to talk about the guilt and explain why he hadn't been able to do the mouth to mouth. Vomit had done something ... and he got back in the car.

What if it had been his son? That's what really kept him awake when things weren't going well and old hurts ganged up on him. Funny that.

When Joanne ran off with that drug artist and they didn't hear from her for two months and the police feared she was dead, he hadn't slept for days and he couldn't help feeling it was God's revenge.

Father O'Leary said God would punish those who did not admit their sins.

'If you tell anyone our secret they won't believe you and you will have committed a sin,' he would say. 'And I won't hear your confession if you tell, and then you'll be damned.'

So, he never told, except that one time to Mother. And the next day he said the story was just an effort to get out of bible study.

He never gave voice to the rest. That sometimes O'Leary would arrive drunk with no bible in his hand. Instead he had the magazines, and he liked to watch Jack reading them.

And the priest would talk about his own childhood and the beatings on his naked body and the grandmother who did terrible things to him. Once he let slip he was having an affair with a married woman and Jack was sure it must be Mrs Prendergast the English teacher because, although her husband was the school librarian, she flirted with the older lads.

Good kid, Joanne. Came back, got married to a publisher and finished her medical degree. And Martin and Jack Jnr, good boys to make a father proud.

Africa reminded him of the Grand Canyon. Not rocky like the Colorado Valley, but the scale of things. Engineering was about building and he'd worked on stadiums, dam walls, bridges and the Trump Tower, but all the engineers of the world with all the equipment and a thousand years to do it couldn't produce a Grand Canyon or a Table Mountain, or Victoria Falls.

The young African guide had all the stats. 'The falls are 5,555 feet wide - that's 1850 yards or well over a mile - and as high as there are days in the year, 365 feet,' he said.

The others were taking pictures but Jack wanted to hear every detail.

'And 56 million gallons of water fall over the precipice every minute, nearly a million per second.'

Jack took out his calculator. When Hoover Dam was built in 1935 it took the Colorado River two years to fill the reservoir, and he punched in some figures. This flow could fill it in two months.

The party from the hotel was snapping like a

fashion shoot though you couldn't hear the clicks. They were at the edge now and the roar of water killed all other noise and he and the guide just smiled at each other as Jack took in the spectacle.

A statue of David Livingstone - the first white man to see the falls - looked across the gorge and the words he had used were inscribed on the plinth.

'A sight so lovely it might have been gazed upon by angels in their flight.'

The plane had levelled out now but the hostess left the mask on Jack's face and that suited him. Less embarrassing. Maybe the other passengers would think he really was ill if he stayed on oxygen.

He had been ill. Cancer scare five years ago; had to take it easy, even now. Made enough money, though they had to be careful, but no real worries. More time had led to the affair with Deborah. Not so bad if she hadn't been Margaret's sister; though in the end, Margie's anger was spread evenly between them both so he hadn't got the full force of it.

But that was behind them. Funny that Margie hadn't come over when she saw he was still on oxygen. Perhaps she was in her personal heaven, the middle seat, where she could chat with two people at once. Only woman he could ever love. Really love. Told her that the night at the Falls when they had done it twice. Surprised her with his stamina. Surprised himself too.

From there the train had gone through Zambia and into East Africa, terminating at the Indian Ocean port of Dar es Salaam. Then, they travelled inland by Jeep to the Serengeti Plain, 18 hours on a rough road, but at least it wasn't flying.

Tall Maasai cloaked in red blankets and carrying eight-foot hunting spears, their faces streaked in white clay, chased cattle out of the way as the vehicle approached.

The country was green but not lush like New England. 'Not an ounce of fat in the land,' Karen Blixen had written in her book, *Out of Africa*. He could see what she meant.

They arrived at the lodge at night and, after a bath and supper he felt a great sense of calm. As if this place had been waiting for him all his life.

The next morning they went out for a game drive at dawn. The Serengeti covered 5,000 square miles of savannah, broken only by flat-crowned acacia trees and the occasional rocky outcrop, and everywhere you looked there was game.

The brochure said there were a million wildebeest and half a million zebra and even those numbers seemed short. They drove in a giant circle for two hours without an end to the herds and, when there was a space, it was filled with giraffe, elephant and prides of lion.

When they pulled up at the last pride, he saw a shadow racing over the ground and looked up to see a hot-air balloon moving silently through the cloudless sky.

'You're mad,' said Margaret when he told her back at the lodge over lunch. 'You'll be terrified up there. I'd be terrified up there and I don't have your phobia.'

'It's not the same,' said Jack as Margaret rose from the wicker chair and, throwing her hands in the air, walked back to the buffet, stopping at two other tables for a chat.

The first blast of flame splashed into what looked like a cloth aircraft hangar as the envelope of the balloon lay on its side in the dark. It was cold on the plane at four in the morning and Jack, Margie and the couple from Sydney, who were also on this flight, queued up for more coffee from the urn on the back of the Jeep.

Slowly, like the monster from a jerky old horror movie, the balloon assumed the vertical and swelled out at the sides as the gas burner heated the air in the envelope, lifting it high as a three-storey building and righting the basket

Ian Rutledge, the stocky tanned captain in his late twenties, did his preflight checks, then called them on board.

'All those who want to come, climb over the wall of the basket.'

'Margaret on this side, Jill, Peter, you take those corners and Jack you're over there. That should spread the weight evenly.'

While the others hesitated - mostly in farce - Jack hauled himself aboard and held his hand to Margie and then to Jill and Peter as they tumbled into the capsule.

The basket gave a little jump, shuddered and then lifted silently from the turf. A minute later Jack was looking down on Eden.

The plains stretched to the end of space, and animals covered the earth. A herd of elephants flapped their ears at the noise of the burner. Then a thermal caught the balloon and pushed it up while a breeze carried it forward and the basket traced a vector across the sky, but the engineer in Jack had taken leave and the child looked down in wonder.

Wildebeest were by far the dominant species and grazed like small, dark cattle. The zebra weren't far behind and looked elliptical from overhead. Giraffe stretched their necks to the tops of the flat-crowned acacias and a pod of hippo slept lazily in a river that flowed into a lake of rosé wine.

As the balloon crossed the lake, the surface of the water came away and Jack thought the flamingos looked like a quilt floating below the basket. The sun reflected off their bodies and for a moment even the air turned pink.

Jack felt the wheels of the aircraft come down for landing, but none of his usual fear. Maybe it was the oxygen, maybe he was asleep. Yes, he should sleep during the landing and imagine he was back on Serengeti. That's where he wanted to be. Back in the basket, but only with Margaret this time so they could make love up there.

That was it. He'd take his licence in flying balloons and stay here forever, flying tourists Monday to Friday and Margaret on weekends, just the two of them.

The Cessna taxied into Dar es Salaam and the ambulance crew were waiting. As they opened the door, the nurse's face told it all.

'We lost him,' she said as the doctor crouched next to the medical bed at the back of the plane.

'What happened?' asked the doctor.

'Balloon ruptured at 800 feet over Serengeti and they fell like a stone. This man, his wife, and two Australians.

'He was the only one with life signs, but he never regained consciousness.'

In the basket, Jack was just about to unclip Margaret's top when he saw another balloon to the right and he pretended to be brushing something off her blouse. Can't have strangers believe they were up to tricks. Not at their age, in a balloon of all places.

There were two people in that basket as well and

they were waving. Heavens above, it was Mother and Father O'Leary. Who would have thought?

He waved back and sent a burst of flame into his envelope and they lifted into the sky where prying eyes couldn't see and he put his arms around the most beautiful woman in the world.

Over her shoulder he could see the expanse of Serengeti and something told him he would never be afraid again.

Geoff Hill

It's In The Stars

Having persuaded her husband Ian to go to their new neighbour's housewarming party for an hour, Jenny went home after two hours, alone.

Ian followed later, singing, 'You were made for me, everybody told me so. You were…Shush!' Opening the bedroom door, he whispered, 'Jen? Are you asleep?'

'I was!' Jenny snapped.

'Why didn't you tell me you were leaving the party?' Ian said, creeping into the bedroom.

'Because you were preoccupied with a busty brunette.'

'Was she busty? I didn't notice.'

'Like hell, you didn't!'

'Now, now, there's no need to be jealous,' Ian said, 'we were only chatting.'

'She was chatting you up!'

'Don't be silly. She simply asked me what my star sign was.'

'You don't believe in star signs,' Jenny mocked.

'I don't, but Ellie does and she knew all about my sign.'

'I bet she did!' Jenny said sarcastically. 'And did Ellie tell you that you were typical of your sign - strong, intelligent, good looking?'

'She did actually,' Ian said, with a self-satisfied grin.

'Well, it's comforting to know that some things never change. 'What's your star sign?' is the oldest chat-up line in the book.'

'You used it on me actually,' Ian said, climbing into bed.

'I did not.'

'Oh yes you did. You said I had animal magnetism.'

'Good God,' Jenny said, laughing. Cuddling up to Ian, she whispered, 'Good night, tiger.'

'Grrrrrrr!' he replied.

Madalyn Morgan

Postcard From Tom

Thank you dear
It was nice to hear
From you
Again

And thank you for the e-mail
Brief, but that's because
Of all its photo attachments
From your holiday in Oz

Twenty-two out of forty-four pics
The others to follow on disc (Oh joy)
Yes I'll look forward to that arriving
Forty four photos of trains on sidings

You've been a friend for so many years
Since the first day at Senior School
But we never went trainspotting together
As far as I can recall

So where are the photos of the cities and towns,
The snow-capped mountains and misty green downs,
The interesting people you must have met?
So why is it just the trains that I get?

E. E. Blythe

White Island

A steaming cone seen from the sea,
a grey desert from the shore,
a hellfire cauldron from the crater rim.

Fish thrive in the warm water
round its base, a paradise for divers,
but a permit is required for landing.

It doesn't look promising.
A few derelict buildings cluster
near the old wharf.
The air reeks of sulphur.

We must follow our guide,
stay on the faintly indicated path,
tread carefully.
Steam rises from fumaroles
rimmed with yellow crystals
on the slope up to the crater.

An inferno, biding its time,
glowing lava churning in its belly,
a bubbling furnace
coughing up boulders -
great globules of molten rock
black against the flames.
White Island.
Awesome.
Waiting.

Wendy Goulstone

The Horsemen

She took in a long breath of the fresh, clean air and cherished the peace she felt settle in her soul. The sun was gently climbing over the tops of the hazy mountains that surrounded her valley - her little bowl of paradise - so she calculated it was roughly 11 in the morning. A breeze whispered in the trees, too gentle to have the strength to push her windmill to action.

No matter, the gush and gurgle of the fast-flowing stream behind her cottage reassured her she would have enough water-generated power for a warm bath for her aching body and her solar panel store was still full from the day before, should she need any extra. She had already finished her morning chores. Goats herded and milked. Pigs fed. Chicken eggs gathered from the hiding places she knew of and could reach. Sweet honey collected. Her stomach grumbled – definitely breakfast time. She plodded back to the kitchen.

She had no idea what the date was, but by the length of the days and the light chill in the air, she guessed it was Autumn.

Autumn meant one thing. A bitter taste rose in her mouth as she thought about having to start up the laptop gathering dust in the cupboard. A necessary evil. The price she agreed to pay for living in her bubble away from the grey and hate and the violence out there in the world. A promise made to touch base once a year with her brother. She wondered if he would even remember if she didn't bother – but she didn't dare, plus, she had made a promise. This was her haven. She hadn't seen another living person for nearly seven years. Her books, her animals and her ghosts kept her company and that was just how she liked it.

'Morning, Micky.' Her voice sounded odd and out of place. An intruder to the silence of the morning. Micky grinned back at her from behind his frozen glass prison on the kitchen table. She picked up the picture frame and kissed his smiling face. He would have loved this place. A thought process she went through every morning. A ritual of grief that she couldn't bear to shake off. He would have been fourteen now. He would have had so many ideas for this place. But then, if he hadn't been taken from her, she would never have come here. How different her life would be.

She ate homemade toast smothered in goat's milk butter and honey, two hard boiled fresh chicken eggs and a little nibble of the last of her stash of chocolate, as she waited for the laptop to whir into life. She had noticed some wild garlic growing at the edge of the forest at Honey Field whilst she had been collecting the sweet nectar that morning and that her tomatoes were ripe – Bruschetta for lunch.

With a sigh she clicked open her email. This reminder of the outside world made her skin itch. Her inbox was full of crap. She ignored it all and began typing.

Dear Alex,

Another year. Not much to report. All is good with me. Last winter was pretty mild so stocks of food, water and electric are high ready for this year which I have the feeling will be harsher, but I'm not worried.

The backfield is cleared now so next spring I will start planting some of those other grains at last. Be nice to have some different bread!

166

Unfortunately, Daisy did not make it. Wolves found their way here last spring. I chased them off before they did too much damage but one got a good bite of Daisy's leg. It became infected and I had to put her out of her misery. I miss the cow's milk but I still have the goats and it has been nice to have a meat option for dinner for a while.

The mild winter and hot summer has got the mountain snows melting more than usual. Good thing because my little brook would be dried up without it I suspect. For now there's enough of a flow to load up the generator regularly with a little help from Mr Wind.

A little worried about the bees. I only have one hive left as the others didn't return this spring. But they still produce more than enough sweet honey to keep me happy. I am sure they'll all come back next year.

Everything else is much like it was. How are you and the girls? Is Emily enjoying Uni still? Send Mum and Dave my love please.

Angie xx

Not much for a years' worth of news. From experience, she knew he would reply within an hour and they would have a little pleasant conversation for a while before he started hinting to her that is was time to come home. She went to have a bath.

An hour later and still no reply. She wasn't too worried. He had a busy life.

She felt it before she heard it. A thump, thump, thump that echoed in her ribcage before it echoed around her valley. The massive helicopter landed in the backfield scattering her animals in a wild panic. Four men – two suits, two army - were disgorged from the noisy machine before it had even stopped spinning its blades and they ran hunched over straight for her house.

Rage was all she felt. She grabbed the shotgun off the shelf and charged to meet them.

'Ma'am?' The two in front wore suits and black ties. Hands up in front of them, fingers splayed. 'Ma'am please put the gun down. We are not here to harm you.'

She kept the gun trained on the older man in the front, he seemed in charge. The tiniest flick of his hand and the two army men broke away and headed towards Honey field.

'Ma'am please put the gun down.'

'Who are you? What are they doing?' The two army men were heading straight for her beehives. She saw they both carried cases and were quickly putting on hive suits as they ran.

'Ma'am, we work for the government. I am going to reach into my jacket slowly and get my badge. Okay?'

She nodded. He showed her his badge. FBI. She lowered her gun.

'What's going on?' She started towards Honey Field.

'Ma'am?' He stepped in her way. 'Please wait here and we will explain everything.'

By the sudden tilt of his head she assumed the excited shout also came through his ear piece, but she could hear it clearly across the valley.

'Sir, it's a beehive. Fully functioning, with a queen.'

Everything changed in a heartbeat. More army men jumped down from the helicopter with hive travel crates and ran towards Honey Field. The suits in front of her dropped the friendly act like a curtain.

'Ma'am, please gather your most essential items, you are coming with us.'

'What? I am not going anywhere. And what are you doing with my bees?' Before she could raise her gun again the old man had taken it from her in a blur of movement.

'Ma'am, we are taking your bees and you are coming with them. It is a matter of national security. Go and pack up your stuff. *Now.*'

The younger suit behind him ushered her into the house. She stood in her kitchen at a loss.

'Ma'am? Now.' This suit was less intimidating but still as forceful.

Another rumbling noise. She felt it come up through the ground. Engines revving, vehicles traveling fast... heading here?

'Sir, we have incoming.' The shout came as the familiar pop, pop, pop of gunfire she remembered from her army days filled the air.

'No time.' Suit had her by the arm and began dragging her out of her cottage. She remembered some of her training and used the element of surprise to wrench out of his grasp. She grabbed Micky and the laptop. Before he picked her up bodily and ran towards the chopper.

'Cover me.' He demanded as he ran and she glanced up to see several army clad men setting up barricades and providing cover fire against three large tank-like vehicles parked across the dirt road into her valley.

She was dumped unceremoniously into the chopper.

'Stay here, buckle up, when we leave it will be fast.' He grumbled at her and took off, sliding the door shut behind him.

Her heart was pounding. She had little tremors

that ran through her body uncontrollably. She couldn't seem to focus on one thought. She was clutching her photograph of Micky to her chest so tightly her fingers hurt. She could hear gunfire going off all around her beautiful valley. Her poor animals must be petrified.

'What the hell is going on?' She needed to escape. Her laptop. Internet still working. Alex.

Still no reply. But then she saw she had several messages from him, mixed up in all the junk. Quickly she did a search and pulled them up. Four in total dated throughout the year. Why would he do that?

Angie
I know you probably won't get this until next year when you decide to open your laptop again. Things have changed. I guess I should have told you when we spoke last but you hate the world so much already.

We are moving away. California is a desert. The rain hasn't fallen here since you went into hiding. We cannot go on with this drought. The girls and I are heading inland to Chicago. Remember Daniel from school? He lives there and reckons he can set us up with a job. I will send you our new address when we are settled (not that you'll ever need it). Keep safe.

Alex xx

Angie
The girls and I only stayed in Chicago for a few weeks. There are food shortages across the country. The government's issued rationing and the riots in Chicago were too dangerous for us.

I am getting Mum and Dave to join us in Ohio. There were hardly any crops this year Angie. The government has this plan for genetically modified stuff but they fed it to the cattle and most of them got sick and died. The drought is all over the country, we're only allowed one litre of water a day. Fires have taken out most of the west coast. Smoke and toxic gas clouds reach all the way to Utah and it's spreading. People are coming East in droves. It's chaos.

Angie it's spring and there's hardly any flowers. It's illegal to pick flowers, can you imagine that?? Suzanne has had to close up her shop, the government is closing florists all over the country, probably all over the world. She is going to join us here. Angie, I am worried. I hope some sixth sense makes you open your laptop early. Please get in touch.

Alex xx

Angie
Please get in touch. Mum, Dave and little Izzy are gone. Listeria of all things. Suzanne never made it to us. I have no idea what happened to her.

It is the end of days Angie, my heart is broken but I keep going for Emily. Wish I knew where you were.

Please get in touch x

Angie
I found Emily and me a place. A farm in a valley just outside Memphis. It was a lovely community, about 25 of us, it was like a big family. We built this big central cabin we all slept and ate in. They had a deep spring so we got fresh water. One of only three places left in the world – in the world Angie – to have bees and other pollinators. They had fields and crops, and flowers – it was so nice to see flowers again Angie. It was so amazing Angie. I wish we had found it in time for the others.

But then they came in the night. Guys with tanks. I

171

was sleeping out under the stars – you remember Angie, like when we were kids – it was so hot. I should have been in there too. They burnt it all down, Angie. With everyone inside. Everyone except me. The government came, but they were too late and really outnumbered.

They stole the bees. They killed them all for the bees. Bees, of all things. There's no bees left in the world and now there's no food and no flowers and no rain. Who knew...bees would be the horsemen of the apocalypse.

I wish it would rain, Angie. It's too dry to cry.

Alex xx

Terri Brown

OverKate

It started so long ago at a time of great hope for me and my family somewhere on the run-down side of Worcestershire in the late 70s.

We had just moved house. We had just moved our colour telly to the first floor lounge and settled down to watch the late-night Midlands programme *Saturday Night at The Mill.*

I was mesmerised by the gyrations of the already famous Kate Bush. That particular track was always a highlight for me and it's called *Moving* but already alarm bells should have been going off because my female family members were less than diplomatic about their feedback on her performance and the recent number one hit *Wuthering Heights.*

'Like a cat locked away from the Kattomeat'
'Like a cat two doors down locked out'
'Like two cats in a bag'
'Like a cat's tail being stepped on'
'Like a cat calling for his cat girlfriend'
'Like a shrieking-cat contest'
'Like a banshee imitating a cat'.

But, like many 16-year-old men, boys really, I took precisely zero notice, even to the extent of going to one of the legendary Kate Bush live concerts all those decades ago. This pattern continued for, I am ashamed to say, many years: my friends being either lukewarm to Kate's appeal or trying to dispel the enchantment cast so long ago.

The divergence between my friends was definitely on gender lines: my male friends seemed to look down their noses on my affection and my female friends - some I could actually call girlfriends - made some inroads into my KB Fantopia. My psychologist female friend suggested there might be a, how to say it, Freudian element to the choruses of an apocalyptic song *Breathing* with the lyric: 'In, out, In, out, In, out,' prominent.

Another actual, girlfriend recounted a story to me of how Miss Bush was nowhere near as cool as she was painted.

However the magical glamour, the spell, was really broken by the song siren herself. Looking back, the quality of the tunes had always been variable right from *Kick inside* to *Eat the music*.

Many clues had always been strewn about like;

- disinterest in touring,
- slow album production,
- derivative melodies,
- occasional cringey lyrics and, at least at first,
- a reluctance to leave the establishment label of EMI.

For the uninitiated, this is the dusty home of such greats as Cliff Richard, The Goons and Five Finger Death Punch. The pattern was of a gradual descent punctuated by tracks of dazzling originality such as *The Dreaming* and *Sat in your lap*.

My disillusionment with *The Red Shoes* was topped with a long wait for the album *Ariel* and, although I have a mathematical training, I have little interest in listening to the number pi quoted to an unlimited number of decimal places. Similarly, I enjoy watching the coloured washing around the machine almost as much as an 18-month-old baby but I really don't want to hear about it on a CD of increasingly low value.

Without making myself look too fickle, there is something about a decade's wait for the new album which can make you slightly less enthusiastic about an artist. So, topped up with this burgeoning indifference and a new life as a married father, I started to cool my ardour towards Kate and grow up.

Finally, the last straw in 2018 was her endorsement of the widely-discredited maybot - Theresa May to you.

Recently her standing has improved, particularly with many female artists, which perplexes me. If I could have the time again, would I just want to exchange the experience and have been a more dedicated indie rock fan?

Would I have been more aware of the marketing hyperbole? Does it really matter? As long as you're not afraid to feel? ('moving' again).

Perhaps, never mind. You can't put old taste in young ears.

Chris Wright

Crying Wolf

Dougie, Dougie, I'm drowning.
I stepped back and bobbed down
And the American Indian boys dived into the Minnesota
River to save me.

What fun it was, I'll do it again.
But Dougie, Dougie, was all I said, when,
Like Alice, I disappeared down a hole.

Gasping. Hands flailing. And feet treading water
My nose and mouth filled. Then, I gave in.
I felt calm. Still.

I was the river now, and the river was me.
Caressing me, seducing me with, its pull and sway,
I waited for Neverland.

Then, whoosh! I was plucked from the water.
Pulled by my hair, my arms,
And dropped like a stone on the shore.

I can hear voices. Blows rain down on me.
My chest is hurting.
I'm sorry, I say.

She's alive! Everyone cheers!
They hold me, hug me, and kiss me.
Then my aunt told me off, and I cried.

Madalyn Morgan

Dipping and Diving

Birds are flocking overhead, dipping and diving
In a formation, dropped away, back together
Where are they going? Where have they been?

Thousands of blackbirds, too small for starlings
Or are they? A flock, a murmuration?
Difficult to see dipping and diving.
They're overhead, flitting over houses

They've disappeared, dipping and diving
Now they've returned these small black birds
What birds can they be, in mid-February?
They are blackbirds, dipping and diving.

Kate A. Harris

Listen Dot, Listen

For Steve, wherever he is now

I always thought that you would be there
I thought you would always be here
I put my trust in you
I loved you
I had faith
I love you

Too little time, it seems to me
That we sat side by side
That we looked at the world the same way
Not enough time
Never enough time

And Oh, I could do with you now
To tell me I'm going to be OK
To say 'Listen Dot listen'
And hold me
And scold me
And mend me

E. E. Blythe

More Tea, Dear?

Marjorie heard her son Gerald coming down the stairs and poured him a cup of tea.

'How do you manage those steep stairs Mother?' Gerald said, entering the sitting room, 'they're lethal.'

'I'm used to them, dear,' Marjorie replied, handing him his tea.

'This house is like a barn. It's freezing up there.'

'That's because I have turned off the central heating radiators in the bedrooms,' Marjorie said.

'Why on earth did you do that, Mother?'

'Because I don't need them all on, and because they are expensive.'

'But you must keep the house aired. If damp sets in, no one will want to buy it.'

'Well that's all right then because I have no intention of selling,' she said. 'Would you pass me my knitting?'

'Mother?' Gerald handed her the knitting. 'You know that new residential place for the elderly I told you about?'

'Nursing home!' Marjorie corrected.

'Well, yes... Anyway,' Gerald went on, 'there's a vacancy and it sounds lovely. There are no stairs to climb, it has underfloor heating at no extra cost, and there's a warden on call twenty-four hours a day. I was wondering...?'

'My neighbour went to live in a place with underfloor heating and it gave her ulcers,' Marjorie said, concentrating on knit-one-pearl-one. 'How anyone can live in one room I'll never know. Where do they put their furniture? And, a busy-body poking their nose into your business day and night?' she tutted. 'It wouldn't do for me!'

Lifting her head and smiling broadly at Gerald, Marjorie said, 'More tea, dear?'

Madalyn Morgan

Perchance to Dream

Dinah woke, suddenly, cocooned in the familiar darkness of her bedroom, the glare of the streetlights shut out by the heavy velvet curtains that formed a black hole against the light walls. Outside it was raining and she pulled the blankets closer round her, glad she didn't have to get up early any more. Warm and comfortable, she listened to the rain pattering on the window panes, a rhythmic counterpoint to the soft breathing next to her.

She froze. Someone was there, in her bed, beside her. She held her breath, listening, afraid to open her eyes. Her heart beat faster. She couldn't breathe out, she couldn't do anything. Fear held her tight, a great, big weight pinning her down.

She was too scared to move. She couldn't put the light on without disturbing the intruder and the telephone was downstairs. Where was her mobile? She opened her mouth to scream, but nothing came out. Who would hear? Who would save her? She was rigid, listening to the soft sounds, trying not to breathe too loudly. Was he really asleep? Was it really a 'he'? Then she was dragged down into blackness, swirling round and round until she was sucked into a whirlpool of oblivion.

In the morning, Dinah woke alone. The terrors of her nightmare had faded with the night. She felt a little foolish. It was just one of those weirdly vivid dreams when you think you're awake, but you're not, she decided. Maybe she shouldn't have had cheese on toast for supper.

Nevertheless, before she did anything else, Dinah checked that her most treasured possessions were still there: the pearl necklace and ruby brooch that Harry had given her on their pearl and ruby wedding anniversaries; the silver framed photograph of their wedding day that always stood beside the bed, the frame a silver wedding present from their daughter Sheila. Dinah sat down, holding the photo. Harry looked so handsome in his best suit and so young, fresh-faced and nervous, standing beside her full of pride and happiness. Next month was their golden wedding and he wouldn't be there. Isn't it supposed to get easier? she asked herself. I miss him more every day.

Ignoring the tears in her eyes, Dinah put the things away and went downstairs for breakfast. Her handbag was hanging on its hook in the coat cupboard. Her cheque-book and credit cards were all there, but she still took out her purse and counted the money. Then she swept the dream out of her mind. The day passed as usual, feeding the cat, doing a little housework, making a quick trip to the shops. The dream was forgotten until bedtime, when, a little embarrassed, she checked that the doors and windows were locked.

She woke in the dark. It was there again. The same gentle breathing sounds next to her, the same feeling that she wasn't alone. For a moment she froze, but then her common sense re-asserted itself. Can't fool me, I'm asleep and dreaming, Dinah thought as she turned over and went back to sleep.

When she made her bed the next morning, she saw that the left pillow was all scrunched up. Dinah had always slept on the right and still did, even though Harry was gone. She trembled as terror slithered into

182

her mind, wriggling round her thoughts and filling her with panic. Someone, or something, had been there. But that's impossible, ridiculous, she told herself. It was only a dream. I must have rolled over during the night. Anything else is nonsense.

The locksmith arrived later. He changed every lock, put window locks on the windows, chattering all the while.

'Better safe than sorry, eh? Always a good idea to change your locks when you first move in. You'd be surprised how many people don't. Asking for trouble, that is. Here's your new keys. Better leave a spare with your neighbour or your daughter. Don't want you locking yourself out, do we?'

He handed her an invoice and left. She felt safer, if a little bit ashamed of her reaction to a stupid dream. Fancy being so scared by a silly nightmare at my age, she thought. I'm not like that. I don't even read the horoscopes. Practical and down-to-earth, that's me. Doubting Dinah, Harry used to call me.

Nevertheless she didn't give a key to her neighbour and she couldn't give a key to Sheila. Sheila lived in Australia with her husband and children. It was at times like this that she really missed her daughter, but she couldn't afford to ring Australia just because she'd had a nightmare. Sheila had wanted her to go with them when they emigrated, but Dinah had refused.

'I don't want to be a burden,' she'd told Sheila, not listening to her protests. 'And besides, I can't leave your father. Who else is going to visit him? Or take flowers?'

On days like this she wished she had gone. It would have been nice to watch her grandchildren grow up. Sheila Skyped every week and on birthdays and Christmas. It wasn't the same though. The time difference made it difficult to have a proper chat.

Sheila's husband was a good man; Dinah approved of him and they got on well. But she was too stubborn and too proud to admit that she could possibly change her mind.

Dinah went to bed that night, thinking of Sheila and her family in the bright, warm sunshine of Perth, while she faced another dreary, gloomy English November. No strange sounds and no strange visitors bothered her and she slept well. She thought the dream was gone, but the intruder returned the following night, breathing quietly and evenly next to her. Paralysed by her fear, not even able to speak, she waited for something to happen, anything, even something bad, as long as she was freed from her nightmare. When she couldn't stand it any longer, a wave of unconsciousness rolled over her and she sank into the safety of a dreamless sleep.

It was becoming more and more difficult to convince herself that it was only a dream. The burglar alarm cost more than she could afford, but she hoped it would bring her peace of mind. Each room had a sensor, a small red eye blinking in the corner, ready to scream at the slightest movement. It made no difference to Dinah's visitor. He was there again beside her the very same night. The new expensive alarm stayed mute and Dinah was frozen by the same panic; she couldn't move, she couldn't even open her eyes.

The next night she left the light on, but she still woke in darkness, hearing him breathe and her own heart race. Slowly she turned her head towards him, determined to find out who, or what, was there. But before she could see, a curtain of darkness descended between them and she was immediately asleep. In the morning she found the light bulb had burnt out.

What am I going to do? she asked herself. There's no-one I can tell. Harry's gone, Sheila's on the other side of the world, most of my friends are dead. I suppose I should go and see the doctor and ask her for some sleeping pills, but I know what she's like. She thinks anyone over seventy is senile and can't look after themselves. She'll have me in a home as quick as a knife. Or I could go to the police. Excuse me, officer, but there's a mysterious man in my bed every night. He doesn't do anything and I can't describe him, because I fall asleep every time I try and sneak a look. I can just imagine. It'd be the loony bin for me. What about Freda? No, she'll only make jokes about people living on their own who drink too much and start seeing things.

Then Dinah laughed. Of course, what a good idea. Before going to bed that night, she finished off the bottle of whisky that had been gathering dust in the sideboard. She had never really liked Scotch, she preferred gin, but, nevertheless, it did help, a little. It didn't make him go away, but Dinah just didn't care. In the morning she felt so ill that she couldn't face repeating the experience. Shouldn't have to get blind drunk to go to bed in my own house, she mumbled through her hangover. It's not right. Why me? Who is he? What does he want?

Her fear was beginning to evaporate. Nothing had happened to her. He was just there, that's all. Didn't speak, didn't do anything. Her night terrors were being swept away by a rising tide of irritation. Dinah knew no-one would ever believe her. They'd think I was so desperate for a man that I'd made one up, she thought. Right, that's it. I'm angry now. I've tried everything and spent most of my savings. I will not be afraid anymore.

I've had enough.

When she woke in the dark, he was there, but this time Dinah was determined. She was not afraid and he was not going to win. She stretched out a hand slowly and carefully towards the bedside light. She had nearly reached it when something touched her. Her body snapped to attention and her heart beat faster and faster. My God, she thought, he's holding my hand! I'm having a heart attack! I'm going to die! Somebody help me! The hand stroked her arm slowly and gently, soothing her as if she were a frightened child. Her heart slowed and she relaxed, calmed by his soft touch. As she fell asleep, it seemed to her that this had happened before. She knew that touch.

Everything had changed. The next evening she went to bed very early. When she woke, he was touching her, caressing her. It feels so good, she thought. It's been so long since anyone held me. It can't be wrong, can it? One arm was flung over her, holding her. Safe, she realised, he's holding me safe. He came closer, until he was curled round her, holding her tight. I wish he would say something, tell me who he is. If I speak to him, will I break the spell? Will he run away from me? Or will he be an incredibly ugly monster, like in the fairy tales?

In the morning, Dinah went shopping for a night-dress. She went to the hairdresser and had her hair done, even though it wasn't OAP day and she had to pay full price. Before going to bed, she ran a bath, adding the expensive bath-oil Freda had given her last Christmas, the one she'd been saving for a special occasion. And if this isn't special, I don't know what is, she thought, lying back in the warm, scented water.

Then she put on her new pale silk night-gown and

placed lighted candles around her bed. The flickering light flattered her. I almost look young again, she thought as she looked into the mirror. Maybe I am losing my mind, maybe I am a sad, lonely old woman. I know it will have to stop. But I've missed being touched, being held, being wanted. I've been so alone since Harry died. There's no harm in it. If only he would speak to me, just once.

When he came, the candles had blown out. She was eager for his familiar touch, enjoying his kisses and welcoming his caresses, touching him, stroking his warm body, surrendering herself. It was wonderful. Nothing had felt this good since her honeymoon, when she and Harry had explored each other's bodies for the first time. Her desire was so intense that it overwhelmed her.

One by one the candles burst into life, burning brighter and brighter. Blinded by pleasure, Dinah was oblivious to the leaping flames. Then, as her passion soared even higher, fire blazed across the room. The curtains were suddenly billowing sheets of flames, the carpet a fiery sea.

*

The sirens wailed in the night, but Dinah didn't hear them. Once the flames had been drowned, fire-fighters searched the house. In the blackened ruin of Dinah's bedroom, they found the charred remains of two bodies lying clasped together.

Fran Neatherway

Louisa *(it is 1918)*

They say that you're not coming back
But that's no use to me
Their words are hollow drumbeats
Going on eternally
They echo in the night when I cannot find my sleep
They sound out with my tears
Making real all my fears
And they tell me you're not coming home
Anymore

I have a tiny white sapphire
Set in a silver band
It means I'm promised to a man
A wedding planned
Panic takes me sometimes and I cannot find the
strength
To face each lonely day
With my young man far away
But I am one of many
Over here

They say that you're not coming back
And that's no use to me
And neither are their words
Of hollow sympathy
My daughter needs her father, and I need my man
The cold years stretch ahead
I must face it, you are dead
And they tell me you're not coming back
To marry
Me
                                        E. E. Blythe

Fenella Faye

Waiting in the wings before her show,
Queen of burlesque, flamboyant Fenella Faye,
Pulled on her sequined Basque,
Took a drag of her fag
And teetered onto the stage.

Break a leg, the stage manager grunted.
Miss Faye to you, Fenella glared, affronted.
Then, gritting her pearly white teeth,
and standing six feet all,
Fenella found her spotlight, and gave her all.

Madalyn Morgan

Ethiopian Mother

Sunrise. The day already blazing.
Beads of perspiration on her skin,
Her thin cotton shift clings to her angular body.

Back straight, legs aching,
the soles of her leathery feet burn in the sand.
But she will not stop until she finds water.
Only then
will she take the crude ochre pitcher from her head.

At last. The water hole is in sight.
But the stench of filth and fear halts her.
Exhausted she casts her wary gaze.
Should she compete with the lion, wolf and hog?

Amidst a chorus of buzzing flies,
she licks her dry chapped lips.
Tastes the salt of her sweat, and walks on.
The children will have to wait.

Madalyn Morgan

The Alternative

It was an embarrassing conversation. Mrs Donnelly stood at the top of the stairs, blocking the doorway of Rose's cold and shabby attic room with her thickset body, making it obvious by her stance that she didn't believe Rose would have the rent by Friday. Rose could neither close her door nor leave. She had to listen and Mrs Donnelly was enjoying every minute of Rose's humiliation.

'Just look at you. Nothing but skin and bone. You haven't worked for the last month and I've heard you coughing. Your fancy ways haven't done you much good, have they? You know my rules. Rent on the dot or you'll have to leave. I'd like to help you,' Mrs Donnelly shrugged in a way that meant she wouldn't and looked away, not meeting Rose's eyes, 'but I can't afford to subsidise every waif and stray. I've got a living to make too.'

Rose stared at the floor, wishing that she'd left the boarding house after the first week, when she had realised how much Mrs Donnelly despised her. She disliked all her young boarders, but reserved most of her spite for Rose, who was quiet and well spoken.

'I promise I'll have the rent for you on Friday,' Rose said, knowing that she only had two dollars in her wallet.

'By six o'clock then or you'll be out that door.'

Mrs Donnelly sniffed contemptuously and turned to go. Rose listened to her heavy footsteps slowly thumping down three flights of stairs to her warm and comfortable apartment on the first floor, where there were carpets and curtains and a fire blazing in the grate. Rose's room was cold because she couldn't afford to heat it. There was a cheap second hand rug on the cracked linoleum and a flimsy paper blind at the dormer window. Her only decent outfit, two years old now, was hanging on the back of the door. The rest of her clothes were neatly folded in a chest of drawers, not that she still had much, just a couple of skirts and blouses and a jumper. Her coat was spread on the narrow bed over the two threadbare blankets that Mrs. Donnelly provided. She kept her practice clothes and shoes in a small attaché case, all ready for an audition, but she knew she wasn't fit enough yet. The influenza had left her so weak that she was exhausted if she tried to dance more than a few steps.

It wasn't fair. First she'd lost her position and then she'd had to use her savings to pay the doctor. He'd told her that she needed three good meals a day to regain her strength, but she couldn't afford it. Breakfast was included in her rent and she ate everything Mrs. Donnelly served, even if it was usually cold and congealed. Then she would go to the delicatessen on the corner and buy yesterday's stale bread cheap and save it until the evening. It wouldn't have been so bad if her show hadn't been in rehearsal, but that only paid half-rate, so she hadn't been able to save anything before she'd been fired.

All her money was gone. She'd sold her good clothes and pawned the pearl necklace that had belonged to her grandmother. What was she going to do? She couldn't go home; she didn't have the bus fare and nor did her family. How could she go back a failure after her mother had scrimped and saved to pay for her dancing lessons? She had sent money home when she could and she wrote regularly, telling her parents how happy she was and how well she was doing. Her mother still wanted her to come home and work at the canning factory with her sister. Every week in her letters she reminded Rose that Ted Withers was still single and every week Rose remembered why she had left Kenosha. If she'd stayed, she would have been gently pressured into a marriage she didn't want, with a man she didn't like.

She picked up her attaché case and set off in search of a new position. The boarding house was only a few blocks away from the theater district, but the walk tired her and she had to rest to catch her breath. The first two theaters had no vacancies. The third was the Barrymore Theater where Vic Groves was the producer.

'Well, girlie, I'm not convinced you're up to it yet, but if you come by tomorrow morning and show me you've got the stamina, well, I might just have something for you.'

Rose knew of his reputation from other dancers, but she also knew he kept his word. She didn't give herself time to think about it.

'Thank you, Mr Groves.'

Maybe, Rose thought, if she did what he wanted, he might advance her the rent money. She walked swiftly away, head down, sure that anyone who looked at her would know what she was thinking of doing for a job.

She'd had such high hopes when she first came to New York, full of dreams and ambitions, unaware that people did such things. In her rather limited experience if you were a good dancer, you got the part. She hadn't realised at first that your hair had to be the right colour

- one producer had a superstition about redheads - or that you had to have the right friends. Dolly Maguire had soon put her straight.

'It's not what you know, it's who you know,' she'd said. 'You should dye your hair blonde, like mine, and socialise a bit more. Backers like to meet the girls.'

The backers, or angels as she learned they were sometimes called, financed the shows. Their behaviour was far from angelic. Most believed if they put money into a show they were entitled to the chorus girls. And if they put in a large sum then they were entitled to one of the solo artistes or the juvenile lead. The management didn't care as long as the money was there. She'd been horrified to find that one particular angel was only interested in the chorus boys, something she'd never heard of back home in Kenosha, and even more horrified to find that the boys were happy to oblige.

'Well, honey,' Jimmy had confided in her, displaying a new watch and a silk shirt, 'I'd never be able to afford these on my wages. And he's not so bad for an old faggot.'

A loud, strident voice interrupted her thoughts.

'Rose, Rose Weston, wait up, will you?'

She turned and saw Dolly Maguire coming down the front steps of the Hepburn Theatre.

'Dolly, hello.'

Rose had met Dolly soon after she'd arrived in New York. At first Dolly had been friendly, showing her the ropes and keeping her out of the usual scrapes that new girls fell into. However, Rose had realised that Dolly, not too popular with the other girls, liked having someone to show off to; it made her feel important. When the next greenhorn arrived, Dolly dropped her. Nevertheless Rose was grateful to her, knowing that she

194

would have found life much more difficult without Dolly's advice.

'Rose, it's been an age. Come and have lunch with me. There's a great little chop suey house on the next block.'

'Oh, I'm sorry, I can't,' Rose said quickly, not wishing to tell Dolly of her poverty.

'Why ever not? Are you meeting someone else?' Dolly made the simple question sound salacious.

'No.'

'Do you have to be somewhere?'

'No.'

'Then I won't take no for an answer.'

'Dolly, I can't afford it,' Rose said quietly, scarlet with shame and embarrassment. 'I've been sick. I haven't worked for the last month.'

'Oh, is that all? Don't be silly, Rose. It's my treat.'

Dolly took Rose's arm and led her down the block to the Chinese restaurant. The thought of a square meal instead of a greasy, meagre dinner at a cheap diner, and she could no longer afford even that, made Rose swallow her pride and submit to Dolly's invitation. Anyway, she thought, maybe Dolly knows of a position or maybe she can get me into Lost For Love. Lost For Love had been running for eight months and looked to run for another eight. Dolly was senior girl and perhaps she could be persuaded to use her influence.

A waiter showed them to a table by the window and they sat down.

'That's a lovely hat, Dolly. Is it new?'

'Oh yes,' Dolly burbled. 'It's a present from my gentleman friend. He's ever so generous. He gave me this too.' She held out her hand. A diamond bracelet was clasped around her wrist. 'He really knows how to give a girl a good time. Such a gentleman. And he's ever so good looking.'

As she prattled on about champagne suppers at fashionable speakeasies, where society rubbed shoulders with notorious gangsters, Rose realised what was expected of her. For the price of a meal Dolly had paid for her undivided attention and if she wanted to tell Rose all about her new romance, then Rose was obliged to listen.

Dolly talked on and on, barely pausing to eat. The food was good and Rose enjoyed every mouthful. It had been a long time since she'd had a decent meal. The waiter brought them jasmine tea and Rose poured it into the shallow cups. Dolly produced a small silver flask from her purse. She unscrewed the top and looked around furtively before pouring some of the liquid into her tea.

'My Frank gave me this,' she said, waving the flask at Rose. 'Want some? It's good stuff, from Canada, not bathtub gin.'

Rose shook her head, thinking she'd probably need a drink tomorrow before she faced Vic Groves again. Dolly took a sip and then giggled, carefully screwing the lid back on the flask and putting it away in her purse. She continued her room by room description of Frank's apartment.

'There's thick pile carpet everywhere and it's real warm. You can see for miles because it's on the top floor. And there's a doorman and a proper elevator with an operator.'

As she cradled the teacup in her hands, Rose caught a glimpse of the real Dolly underneath, the girl from Hell's Kitchen who had clawed her way out of the slums by sheer persistence and had become as hard as nails on the way. Now she had gotten herself a beau who had a luxurious penthouse and lavished gifts upon her. Impulsively Rose put out a hand.

'Oh Dolly, I'm so pleased for you, I truly am. I hope you'll be real happy.'

Dolly looked at her suspiciously, but she saw the sincerity in Rose's eyes and for a moment she was touched. Not many people had ever cared about Dolly Maguire and she suspected that Frank was not one of them, even though he was generous. She was filled with sudden affection for Rose.

'Thank you, honey,' she said. 'Tell me how you are.'

Briefly Rose explained. 'I have to find the rent by Friday or I'm out on my ear. That's only two days. I don't have much choice really. The only offer I've had is from Vic Groves and you know what that means. You were the one who told me in the first place.' She looked hopefully at Dolly. 'Unless you can...'

Dolly already regretted asking. 'No, no, I never lend money. Anyway I don't have much cash. Frank pays my rent and...'

It was Rose's turn to interrupt. 'No, I wasn't asking for money. I just wondered if you could put in a word for me with your management. If there's a position in the chorus, or an understudy, or even in the wardrobe? I can sew real neat.'

Dolly was gratified that Rose thought she had so much influence. In reality senior girl meant the one who had been there the longest and she had fallen out with nearly everybody. She would have been fired weeks ago if Frank hadn't been one of the more important angels. He liked to watch her dance. Sometimes he would make her dance for him in his apartment, naked except for the jewellery he'd given her. She loathed doing it, but she loved him and if it made him happy, well then, she was happy to do it. The memory of the evening when he had invited half a dozen of his friends to watch was one she had tried very hard to scrub from her mind.

'Well,' said Dolly, 'there isn't anything going at the moment, but I'll let you know the minute there is.'

Disappointment overwhelmed Rose. She hadn't realised quite how much she had pinned her hopes on Dolly.

'Of course,' Dolly continued, 'Frank has friends who would be very happy to take out a girl like you and if she was properly grateful, they'd give her lots of nice presents. I'll talk to him tonight.'

She stood up, relieved that she didn't have to do anything other than tell Frank that she knew this real pretty dancer who was flat broke. He knew the score and if one of his friends took a liking to Rose, there would be a nice present for Dolly. It wouldn't do Rose any harm either to have a bit of fun and make a little extra money. She was looking rather peaky. Pulling some bills from her purse, she dropped them on the table.

'There, that should cover it. Leave a message for me at the theater and I'll introduce you to my Frank.'

She swept out of the restaurant, leaving Rose to finish the tea. She sat in the warmth of the chop suey house, making the tea last as long as possible, wondering what on earth she should do. Vic Groves or Frank's friends? Was that any different than letting Dolly pay for lunch?

The waiter delivered a plate of fortune cookies with the check. Dolly had left enough money to pay it twice over. The restaurant was nearly empty. There was just a couple two tables away and they were far too interested in each other to take any notice of what Rose was doing. Deeply ashamed of her actions, she put half the bills in her wallet and took out two quarters. Then she wrapped up the fortune cookies in her clean handkerchief and put them in her purse for tomorrow. No-one had seen her, much to her relief, and she rose to leave. The waiter came rushing over to help her with her coat. He looked pleased with his fifty cents and Rose felt even more guilty.

She walked slowly back to the boarding house, enjoying the faint warmth of the early spring sunshine. It softened the sharp March wind and almost made her feel optimistic about her future. She felt tired, but she hadn't coughed all day and she believed that she could and would dance again. She stopped at the corner of her block and bought a newspaper.

Back at the brownstone, she crept in quietly, hoping to avoid another encounter with Mrs Donnelly, but as soon as she opened the front door, Mrs Donnelly appeared from the depths of her apartment, like an evil genie from an old and dented rusty lamp.

'Well, Miss Weston, got another job yet? Don't forget your rent's due on Friday.'

'Don't worry, Mrs Donnelly, you'll have your money,' Rose said wearily, all the lightness gone out of her step.

She put one foot on the first stair and started to cough. Her chest heaved with the exertion and tears came into her eyes. She turned away, unwilling to let Mrs Donnelly see.

'I better had or else it's the street for you.' Mrs Donnelly looked at her slyly. 'Unless, of course, you'd like me to introduce you to my nephew. He's always on the lookout for likely girls.'

Rose couldn't believe it. A third person suggesting she should sell herself. Well, maybe they were right, but it wouldn't be to a relative of Mrs Donnelly. She would sooner be homeless.

'Thank you, Mrs Donnelly, but I'll be fine.'

She trudged up the stairs to her attic, thoughts whirling round her head, but finding no solutions. She sat in the lumpy chair beneath the grimy dormer window and opened her newspaper to the Help Wanted section. There wouldn't be any positions for dancers advertised, but maybe it was time to look for something else. There were only a few jobs for women and she didn't have the right experience suitable for any of them. Why hadn't she learnt to type and do shorthand as her grandmother had suggested? She had said that Rose might need an alternative skill one day. And Rose, full of youth and arrogance, had replied sassily that she was going to be a dancer, she didn't need an alternative. Now she was desperate for one.

She lay down on the sagging mattress and pulled the blankets and the coat over her, still fully clothed to keep warm. Tired after all the walking she fell asleep quickly. When she woke, it was dark. She went to the window and looked out at the city, full of light and life. It was still early and her stomach rumbled, lunch long forgotten. She remembered the fortune cookies and decided to allow herself one. The small paper strip fell out as she broke the cookie open and she let it lie on the floor. She ate the cookie as slowly as possible, licking the crumbs from her fingers. Then she wrapped herself up in her coat and went back to bed, where she tossed and turned before falling into a dream-ridden, restless sleep.

*

In the morning, she picked up the fortune and read it. What you desire is always possible. An omen, she thought, and decided she would go and see Vic Groves and explain how much she needed a job. Perhaps he would be sympathetic and not insist on payment in kind. After forcing herself to eat the undercooked bacon, runny egg and the one slice of toast that was all Mrs Donnelly allowed her boarders, she walked as swiftly as she could to the Barrymore Theater. Vic wasn't there and the stage doorkeeper wouldn't let her wait. She met Jimmy on her way out.

'Rose, honey, what are you doing here? Come and have a good old gossip with me, just us girls.'

Rose hugged him. She'd always been fond of Jimmy, once she'd got over the shock of finding he preferred men. Like Dolly, he had helped her learn the ropes, but, unlike Dolly, he was genuinely interested in her.

'Well, honey,' he used to say, 'be nice to everyone on your way up. You never know who you'll meet on the way down. Of course I'm an expert on going down.'

All the other chorus boys had laughed with him.

'You sure said a mouthful, sugar,' one giggled.

Rose hadn't understood either comment and Jimmy hadn't enlightened her. There was something about her innocence that made him feel protective.

He whisked her past the stage doorkeeper, fluttering his fingers and lisping, 'My friend's just popping in for a quick one.'

Sitting in the boys' dressing room, surrounded by sweat encrusted costumes, tap shoes, grease paint and soiled balls of cotton wool, all coated with a thick layer of face powder, Rose felt secure amidst the familiar debris. Jimmy lit a cigarette and passed it to her. She inhaled and then coughed painfully. Jimmy took it away from her.

'I haven't had one for a while.' She looked at her pale face in the harshly lit mirror, too pale under her dark shingled hair. Even her mouth, unadorned by lipstick, was colourless. Her big eyes stared anxiously back. 'Look at me. No wonder I can't get a place. I look as if I'm in the last stages of consumption.'

'What's wrong, sweetie?' Jimmy asked.

Rose told her story again, knowing that this time her listener was genuinely interested.

'As far as I can see, I have three choices and they are all the same. Vic Groves, Frank's friend or Mrs Donnelly's nephew.'

She burst into tears. Jimmy put his arms around her and held her close as she sobbed into his jacket. He was warm and comforting and for a moment the thought crossed her mind that if he were Vic it would be no hardship, but common sense re-asserted itself immediately. No point in compounding her misery by falling in love with a fag. Gradually her tears ran dry and she scrubbed at them with Jimmy's handkerchief, while he patted her on the back.

'Well, honey, I shouldn't choose Vic. Sure, you put out and he'll give you a place - if there is one and I can tell you there isn't. So save it until there is, because I know he'll have forgotten he owes you by then.' Jimmy stood up, stretched and tapped across the room. 'Step, ball change and turn. Dolly's friend Frank. No, no, no, sugar. He runs with a bad crowd. They dope and gamble and some of the girls have ended up in houses and you don't want that.'

GET TO THE POINT

'Houses?'

'You know, of ill repute, madams and all that.' He sighed. 'Sometimes I don't think you should be let out unaccompanied. You remember Anna Harris? Blonde, not much of a dancer, but made up for it in looks.' Rose nodded. 'She got in with that crowd. Now she's in a house in Chinatown. It was the dope that put her there.' He looked at Rose's shocked face. 'Don't worry, hon, it's not going to happen to you. Mrs Donnelly's nephew? Forget it, she probably just wants to scare you into coming up with the rent. How much money have you got?'

Rose turned out her purse. With Dolly's money it came to seven dollars and forty-five cents. Not enough. She needed ten dollars for the rent.

'I'll lend you three dollars while we come up with a plan. Why do you stay there? She's such an old gorgon.'

'It's cheap and it's close by so I don't have to pay bus fare,' Rose said, hugging Jimmy again. 'Thank you so much.'

'That's OK,' Jimmy said. 'I always wanted to save a fair maiden from a fate worse than death.'

*

On Friday at precisely six o'clock, Rose knocked on Mrs Donnelly's door. It opened and Mrs Donnelly's round red face looked out scornfully at her.

'I guess you've come to tell me you can't pay.'

'No,' Rose said and handed over the bills. 'May I have a receipt, please?'

'Oh yes, you may,' Mrs Donnelly sneered and went back into her apartment.

She returned and gave Rose a grubby piece of paper on which was hastily scrawled 'Received $10 from Miss Rose Weston for rent'. With her was a chubby, pasty-faced young man. Rose could see the family resemblance.

'This is my nephew, Gordon,' she said, looking at him fondly.

'Pleased to meet you, I'm sure,' he said, putting out his hand.

Rose shook it. His grip was limp and his palm was clammy. It reminded her of Ted Withers.

'Good evening,' she replied politely.

Mrs Donnelly looked arch. 'He's my favourite nephew. A nice girl without a beau could do worse.'

'Yes,' Rose lied. 'Excuse me, I have an engagement this evening.'

She turned away and Mrs. Donnelly and Gordon went back inside, but the door was not closed properly. Rose could hear their voices and then she heard her own name. She listened. She couldn't help herself.

'I thought you said she'd got no money. Ripe for the picking, you said. Don't look like it to me.'

'I don't know where she got it from. Maybe she's gone into business for someone else.'

'Classy looking broad. And she speaks nice too. I could make a lot of money.'

'Come back next week. She might be broke again.'

Rose had heard enough. She climbed the three flights of stairs to her cold, miserable room and slumped down on the bed. There seemed to be no way out of her predicament unless she was prepared to prostitute herself and she wasn't sure if she could go through with it. The thought of someone like Gordon Donnelly touching her with his clammy hands made her feel sick. Vic Groves wasn't so bad, but he was old, and if Jimmy was right about there being no vacancies, there was no point. As for one of Frank's friends, she remembered meeting Frank once and she hadn't liked him one little bit. There was something nasty lurking behind his eyes and Jimmy's warning had frightened her.

Her stomach growled with hunger; she hadn't eaten since breakfast. She nibbled a fortune cookie slowly, pretending it was a substantial meal, and read the fortune. Be true to your dreams. Yes, she thought, I will not give in. I will find another job. Then she slept.

*

In the morning, she woke, feeling positive about the future. She hadn't coughed for two days now. Even one of Mrs Donnelly's greasy breakfasts did not discourage her. She took her audition clothes with her and went for a walk in the park, enjoying the spring sunshine until it was time to meet Jimmy at the Barrymore.

'Great news, sugar, I think I've found something for you.' Jimmy handed her a business card. 'This guy has a small night-club and he's always looking for girls. Get yourself over there and he'll give you an audition. It's not the theater, but you'll be able to eat until something better comes along.'

'Oh, Jimmy,' Rose said, flinging her arms around him and hugging him. 'Thank you so much. What would I have done without you?'

'Just get the job, honey,' Jimmy said, feeling pleased with himself.

'I'll come back and tell you all about it.'

Rose kissed him on the cheek and hurried off to

the Starlight Club. It was several blocks from the Barrymore, off the main street. As she walked further away from the theater, the area became more run down, less respectable. She turned into the cross-street and spotted the sign over a narrow doorway. Starlight Club. Girls, Girls, Girls. Maybe this is not a good idea, she thought, but do I have a choice?

Inside the club had that tawdry air of being caught undressed that all night places have in the daytime. A middle-aged woman was pushing a broom over the tiny dance floor, a bored expression on her face. Behind the bar a man in shirt sleeves was polishing the glasses. A hand-written notice stated that serving alcohol was against the law.

'Can I help you?' he said, not meaning it for a moment.

'I'd like to see Mr Bonetti, please,' Rose said in a whisper.

'About what?'

'I understand he's looking for dancers?'

'OK, wait here, will you? Do you want a drink?' He produced an unlabelled bottle from under the bar.

'No, thanks.'

'Suit yourself.'

He disappeared into a back room. Rose looked around. There was a small stage in front of the dance floor, the tired velvet curtains pulled back. Beside it were an upright piano, drums and several music stands. Tables and chairs were clustered so closely together that there was hardly room to pass between them. The smell of stale cigarette smoke and alcohol lingered from the night before. She could almost see it.

'I hear you're looking for me.'

Rose turned round quickly. He was leaning on the

bar, a large cigar in his hand. His suit was expensive, the jacket open over his large belly, and his silk shirt was decorated with gold cufflinks and tie-pin. A diamond ring glittered from each pinkie and his black hair was greased back with a strong-smelling pomade.

'Mr Bonetti?'

'That's me. You looking for a job?'

'Yes, I am. I'm a dancer.'

The bartender had returned and was sitting at the piano. Bonetti pointed at the stage with his cigar.

'OK then, girlie, let's see what you can do.'

Rose walked onto the stage. 'Ballet or tap?' she asked.

Bonetti laughed. 'Just high kicks, sweetheart. Can you manage that?'

'Yes, of course I can,' she said. 'Where do I get changed?'

'Just pull your skirt up,' Bonetti said. 'You got nothing I ain't seen before and I need to see your legs.'

Rose was embarrassed, but nevertheless she lifted her skirt a little.

'Higher,' he gestured.

She pulled her skirt up over her thighs, revealing stockings and pale skin. A sick feeling twisted and turned in the pit of her stomach. Her face was almost completely white, apart from two bright red patches on her cheeks. The bartender struck up a tune with a heavy, rolling beat. Rose didn't recognise it, but she began to high kick in time with the piano.

Bonetti had been joined at the bar by two other men, who were staring at her avidly. Their eyes crawled over her body, making her feel dirty, like a slab of meat laid out on display. Bonetti let her continue for five more humiliating minutes before he waved at her to stop. He hadn't even been looking at her; he'd been talking to the men.

'You'll do. I'll give you a week's trial. Be back here at five for rehearsal with the other girls. You'll be expected to sit with the customers between numbers, but any arrangements you make with them are up to you, as long as they buy plenty of drinks.'

Rose walked back to the Barrymore, undecided about the job. It wasn't what she had hoped for, it wasn't even dancing really, and she did not want to make 'arrangements' with the customers, but she needed the money. Perhaps she should do this until something better came along. She would go and talk it over with Jimmy.

At the Barrymore, Jimmy was talking on the telephone. He didn't see her.

'So you liked her then? You think she'll work out? Yeah, I know, that innocent look'll drive 'em mad. No, no, don't worry, she's desperate for money. She's ripe for it. Same commission as usual? Maybe I should ask for a bit extra for a genuine virgin.' He laughed and hung up the phone.

'Hello, Jimmy.'

'Rose, honey, how did it go?'

'I think you already know that,' she said, tears rolling slowly down her face. I thought you were my friend. I didn't realise you were selling me to the highest bidder. No wonder you didn't want me to accept any of the other offers.'

A mixture of shame and embarrassment crawled furtively across his face. He looked away from her and then back.

'It wasn't like that, honey, honestly. Not for the money. It's just that, well, if you were going to do it,

then I thought...What can I say? I'm sorry.' He
brightened. 'I can share it with you. Fifty-fifty?'

'Forget it, Jimmy. Goodbye.'

She turned and ran down the steps. Jimmy called
after her, but she ignored him. He swore and punched
the wall, hurting his hand. Rose hoped he'd broken it.
She would never speak to him again.

*

Back in her room at the boarding house she thought
about her options. The Starlight Club seemed to be her
only choice. When she had left Kenosha last year, she
had never thought she would end up working in a
clip-joint. She hadn't spent all those years at dance
classes for this - high kicks in a skimpy costume,
enticing men to buy expensive drinks. And it wouldn't
be long before she had to do more than drink with the
customers. She thought of Jimmy, the expression on his
face, his greed, and she felt betrayed.

There was still one fortune cookie left. Maybe that
would help her decide. She opened it and read it.
Calmness enveloped her, embracing her in its peace.
Her decision was made. Yes, Rose thought, now I know
what I have to do.

*

In the morning, when Rose hadn't appeared for
breakfast, Mrs Donnelly huffed and puffed her way to
the top floor. She knocked on Rose's door. There was no
reply. Mrs Donnelly turned away. If Rose chose to miss

breakfast, that was her lookout, none of Mrs. Donnelly's concern. Nevertheless something made her knock again.

'Miss Weston, you in there? You missed your breakfast.'

She pushed open the door. Rose lay on the bed, dressed in her dancing clothes, ballet shoes carefully tied with pink satin ribbon. An empty bottle of pills lay in one hand. In the other was a slip of paper. Mrs Donnelly took it from her limp grasp and read it.

There is always an alternative.

Fran Neatherway

Sundays

The idea was to have a leisurely Sunday afternoon drive. I should have known better. There's no such thing as a leisurely drive on a Sunday afternoon, especially when you have a neurotic girlfriend and she has a flatulent dog.

I had somehow managed to call Suzie (the neurotic girlfriend) fat, while discussing the weather, which had resulted in her yanking the car radio's volume button up and off in a fit of anger. The windows throbbed with the teeth jarring volume of the chart show. I could have just turned the radio off but pulsing pop tunes drowned out the sound of ominous silence from the passenger seat.

Honey, (the flatulent poodle) was turning the air inside the car a decidedly mauve colour with her noxious gases. My one attempt at opening the window to let in some breathable London smog air had immediately led to accusations of being uncaring for 'hadn't I noticed that Suzie had a slight chest infection' and I was letting the cold in. All I wanted to do now was get home. But I was stuck behind this moron doing 3 miles a fortnight and actually seemingly enjoying his leisurely Sunday afternoon drive.

I looked at this fellow in front of me through his rear window. His white hair framed the oval bald spot on his gently bobbing head. Fingers tapping slowly on the steering wheel. I imagined him listening to Beethoven or Jazz at a normal volume, a slight smile on his lips, a serene look in his eye as he cruised slowly around the suburban streets, rejoicing in the rustic colours of the trees and the laughter of children... and I wanted to ram him off the road.

I gritted my teeth as another foul smelling cloud wafted over from the back seat and with a growl of frustration, I knew I had to get past this joker in front of me and get home fast before I had some sort of nervous breakdown. I put my foot down and flung the car into the oncoming lane without even looking if anything was coming. Luckily (and rarely for London) nothing was.

Suzie sucked on her teeth and I could feel her gathering momentum for a full onslaught at the childishness of the manoeuvre. All I could see through the red haze that had settled over my eyes was this bozo in the other car having the audacity to enjoy his Sunday drive and every bad thing in the universe was suddenly his fault. I prepared to fix him with a death stare as I accelerated past.

It wasn't until I was level with him that my death ray glare faltered and the red haze faded. I could now see in the back seat of his car, a pile of fur that loosely resembled a dog. I couldn't remember what they were called, but they had always reminded me of aggressive rats on leads whenever I'd seen old ladies dragging their smelly little bodies around town. It was yapping relentlessly at everyone and everything. I even fancied I could hear it through the closed windows and over my radio volume.

In the passenger's seat was a white haired lady. So small and shrivelled I hadn't even seen her. She was in exactly the same stance as Suzie: sitting rigidly in her seat, staring out the window. However, what I then saw made me feel overcome with immense gratitude that I was in this car and not that one, because the little white-haired lady's mouth was going ten to the dozen.

I glanced into my rear-view mirror as I finished overtaking and settled the car in front of him. I fancied my eyes met his eyes for a second. It was not serenity I saw, but resignation. In that brief moment of contact, it was almost as if he spoke to me and I wasted no time in taking his advice.

Suzie was miffed, to say the least, when I broke things off with her, but, last I heard, she was getting married to some harassed looking insurance salesman. I couldn't get the smell of dog out of the car so I sold it and bought a bicycle and now I am engaged to a lovely girl called Helen who owns a very healthy cat and likes taking leisurely Sunday afternoon walks sans pet.

Terri Brown

The Unexpected Visit

It was a normal Saturday in those days: work until midday, and then football. Tom so looked forward to the weekend match and meeting his brothers, arriving home to change and have a quick lunch - but not today. Irene was ready for him, Patricia was in her pram and as usual wanting to be held.

'Come on, Tom, we'll have to hurry, Mum and Dad are coming to visit, the train will be arriving in an hour.'

'But they never visit, and when did they say they were coming?'

'I just know they will be here and they will be coming into Euston.'

'Please Tom! We'll have to hurry!'

'They can't go into Euston. They would only travel on the LNER.'

'Please.'

At long last they set off and arrived at Euston just as the Nottingham train pulled in.

The passengers made their way off the platform, Irene's parents amongst them. Their first words were: 'Oh, did you get our telegram?'

'No,' said Irene.

Just as they all arrived at the house, a telegram was delivered. My mother could always surprise us.

Pam Barton

ZooTropical

BUSH BABY
I'm not even an ape too tiny with big eyes
The tree doesn't strain with a child of my size
The eyes can't stop seeing
Seeing is being
and watching is catching
and if I see it I have to have it
I can't see you my Dear
it's not real if it's not near
Fruit left lonely on a stump?
Look. I can see it! JUMP!

SHEEP
we have a gang we
have each other
All corralled in a housing estate
with middle class, middle aged, Midlanders
They hold brooms across their groins
fencing us
I'm following you, following her, following me
I would find it funny if
there was someone to tell me
whether it is funny
bright orange a cat trying to pass deftly
It escaped. Now we only have ourselves to follow

MAGPIE
I'm hopping outside.
you see me and salute
Annoyance quite mild chipping at the truth

You wish I could go away
and bring the rain cloud back
My wife and I try to bring you back on track

CAT
Is anything as incontinent as me?
I do what I like, you have to like it.
Because I look at you from your neighbour's sofa.
What a silly Idea to throw that boot at me
Because that would be throwing a boot at missus
Brown

LEMMING
I don't want to go
Stop pushing me to the front
I wanted to go left or even would put up with right
Would taking a giant Leap Forward with the cliffs of the
soul
Be taking back control?
If it weren't for my family pinning me in tight
I could have escaped by now The Running Free In The
Night

DOLPHIN
Swims down your High Street looking glumly at the sub
aqua crisp packets and copies of *The Daily Mail* hiding
the barnacles and wonders what happened.

Chris Wright

Tunnel Vision

The hammer drill was killing his head even though it was in the next chamber.

Oktoberfest was for tourists in hotels where breakfast ran to eleven. Not here. Daniel König had been up at dawn, but when you get to bed after midnight, any time is too early, even in autumn when Berlin was dark until 7am and the sun only rose after 8. His head hadn't been so bad then, just tight along the brow. Now it hurt when he swallowed, and his stomach felt like raw fish in custard.

He'd planned to doze on the train, then, worried about missing his stop, picked up the free morning paper another passenger had left on the seat and tried to read, but it made no sense except page 5 where he stared longingly at the ad for a double bed.

At Hauptbahnhof - Berlin's railway palace, covering an area of six football fields near the centre of town - he transferred to a company bus for the airport.

The queue was as dull as the coming winter: the shuffled steps of men shackled to labour at an age when those who had done better in youth could choose their work.

Brandenburg, Berlin's new gateway was on the site of the old East German terminal at the now-closed Schönefeld air base south of the city and half-an-hour by bus.

But passengers would have no such delay: Daniel and a team of drillers, engineers, surveyors, concrete experts and every other speciality were building a tunnel for an underground train that would reach

Hauptbahnhof in just 15 minutes.

He was born in West Berlin when it was a tiny island of freedom surrounded by the Soviet-run Deutsche Demokratische Republik or DDR, and at school when the country was unified in 1990 and the communist east - poor, depressed and inefficient - came back to the Fatherland.

At that time there were three airports:

- Tempelhof, opened in 1923 from where Hitler flew to rallies around the country.
- Schönefeld also from the Nazi era, taken over by the Soviet occupiers after the war.
- Tegel, built in 1948 for the Berlin Airlift when Stalin sealed off West Berlin and wouldn't allow supplies in from the DDR by land, and the Allies flew in everything, until the Russians relented.

There were others including the Zeppelin base at Staaken and smaller airfields used by the British and Americans after the war, but all had been closed in the German push for scale and efficiency. Tegel would be the last to shut, but only once Brandenburg was in full flight: a fitting gateway to the richest country in Europe.

Few could imagine how noisy and dusty it was building a tunnel and, two hours after starting his work of sweeping up the debris with a yard broom, Dan felt close to death. The drill stopped but the throb continued in the jelly of his brain, vibrating against the earplugs that looked like headphones and kept out most of the noise.

He took the bracket off his head, rolled his shoulders and turned his neck from side to side. Silence meant coffee and buns, welcome on any day and more-so when he had skipped breakfast.

There was no time to go up in the lift for a tea-break, and the contractor had agreed that workers would have meals in a chamber off the access tunnel. It was cool and, at a glance, could be taken for a normal dining room, well lit and the earth walls covered in hessian painted over with white-wash.

The lights of the dining hall struck matches; each one flared behind his eyes, then burned along a fuse to the base of his skull and into the shoulders. He squinted and walked to the table, grunting at those who stopped their conversations to greet him, mouths munching and a smirk in their eyes.

"Here comes Mr Sweeper with a Monday face."

Daniel picked a cardboard cup and filled it from the urn. The coffee was hot as a paper-cut and the bun went down like a sponge, sucking poison from his gut and swelling to a lump that pressed on his lungs. A cigarette would have settled the nausea, but the site was smoke free.

He thought of clocking off sick.

"Four times now on Monday, Herr König!" The foreman had not issued a warning last week, but signed the sick-note with a flick of the wrist, then thrust it forward and shook the paper so it rustled, letting go a moment before Dan fumbled and had to pick it off the floor.

Dan left the diner, walked back to the quiet half-light of the tunnel and made his way to where he had been working. Then he branched to last month's diggings and down to the next level and down again to where there was only one light every 200 metres as required by law in case someone strayed and got lost.

The zigzag of gentle slopes had been built to

access the main dig where eventually a train would run to town. For now, that tube was only large enough for trucks to move underground, laying cables and ferrying the engineers and geologists who tested rocks and made calculations to keep the tunnel straight and true.

Some months back he'd sneaked off for a rest and no one noticed, or the work team - worried enough by his mood - had let it go.

Germans, he suspected, had a habit of selling-out their comrades to authority. That's how the Gestapo had worked under the Nazis and the Stasi in East Germany: wives spying on husbands, children on parents and workers on each other. But if he got caught now in the tunnels, he could always say he had shown initiative by cleaning down another line when there were men enough at today's site near the surface.

The mid-point between two lights was best. Dark enough to ease his head and light enough to make out the hue of soil on the walls. The usual scaffolding crisscrossed the passage and buckets, wheelbarrows and hardware sat in well-sorted clumps.

There were ridges in the floor where the soil had not compacted and, while a vehicle could roll over them, they might twist an ankle of those who didn't watch their step.

The tunnel was cool with a hint of damp and, best of all, silent. Teatime was over and the hammer started again, muffled by distance but still too close and he walked on, searching now for an alcove where even a passing truck wouldn't see him.

Dan wasn't sure how many turns he'd made when he saw a storage hall branching off to the right, big enough to hold equipment or park a van. These dead-ends rarely went more than 30 metres. Just as he stopped at the entrance, he heard the sound of a vehicle moving down from the surface.

Dan turned and squinted; no sign yet of headlights, but he could hear the engine three or four levels up. Probably engineers who would no doubt ask if he wanted a lift.

He walked into the cul-de-sac. There were no bulbs here, but glow from the mainline ventured in and he walked to the end, leaned against the wall and waited.

A smell of smoke caught the air. Yes, it was tobacco, quite recent. He paced forward and the scent was gone.

Daniel could still hear the hammer, like blood pumping in your ears when you've run too fast. Then, all was dark and silent. Maybe the power had gone off. There had been problems with electricity because no one was sure how much the project needed, and if the drain was too high, the system shut down. Generators would kick in after eight seconds to run the work zone, but not enough for the tunnels.

"Nothing wrong with that," he thought, and already the pain in his head was less intense.

Scaffolding and the rough floor made it hard enough to negotiate the route; without lamps it was impossible.

He sat down on the earthen floor, took a long breath, then stretched out on his back and felt the dark embrace him like the feathers of a black swan.

The drills started up and he blinked just long enough to see that darkness remained, and heard the vehicle stop, reverse and make its way back.

Loneliness can hurt but solitude is bliss and he felt the stress leave his shoulders and the spongy bread shrink away from his lungs. In that moment, Daniel König felt he could lie here for eternity and never wish to stir.

Just as he got comfortable, the coffee - or last night's beer - swirled in his bladder and, although the pressure was light, it would build and wake him, so better out than in.

He lay a moment more then, with his eyes still closed, pressed on the floor and stood up like a foal on shaky legs. The ballast moved in his stomach and he belched and farted, and the shift made a pee more urgent.

Not even an owl can see in total darkness, and the human eye is far less efficient. Daniel turned, then realised he was no longer sure which way led to the surface. He took two steps and bumped into the side, stepped back, then unzipped his overalls and urinated against the earth wall.

His water smelled as it usually did after a big night, and he turned his head from the rising vapour. There, somewhere near what must be the blunt end of the cul-de-sac was a thin line of gold like a light shining under a door.

He felt the warmth as urine crossed his fingers and went back to the task in hand. Now zipped, he looked again, expecting, as one does, that such an impossible sight will be gone. Not this time.

Still doubting his eyes, Daniel took a small step, then another. There was a line of light, perhaps a metre long, running parallel to the floor.

"Must be a work area behind this one," he mumbled to himself, "maybe a battery lamp inside."

He was about to lie down when the thought struck him that if someone was working in there, they might come out and find a shirking cleaner. But, with the lights still off, he couldn't go anywhere.

There is something about the dark that changes how we walk, as though the next step might send us tumbling into a chasm and he shuffled towards the mirage, holding his hands in front of him as if to clear the way.

Now he knelt and examined the vision. The horizontal line he had seen was the thickest, but at either end of it was a vertical stripe thin as a hair, running up the wall for at least two metres, just the right size for a door.

As he reached out to feel the surface, he heard footsteps on the other side and two men talking. Now a woman's voice, all in German but so muffled it was impossible to pick out the words. Then boots, moving away from the door, walking on a hard surface, cement probably, on and on until they faded.

He moved aside and lay with his back to the wall. The only thing now was to get some sleep and, when he woke more sober, take another look.

At his age, this must be payback.

His doctor had warned him: "Think of it as a drug, Herr König, one that damages not only the liver but the brain."

His wife used to cry when he came home drunk, then hug him when he went dry, and talk about her father who died at 56, his organs bleached with brandy.

Even his sister, when she phoned from Moscow where she was teaching German, spoke of how many Russians had early onset dementia from their love of vodka, but he knew she was talking about him.

The footsteps returned from quite a distance given how long they took to reach the door. Daniel lay still.

"This is the problem I was telling you about." It was a man's voice, with the high-German accent of a bygone era.

"Most unfortunate." Another man now, deep and confident, but again with the clipped tone of his grandfather. "Tell me captain, do you think they saw anything?"

"No sir. We calculated the tunnel would run parallel to our rooms. What we didn't anticipate are these side passages, but only this one shaved the border. As you know, when they dig here we turn off our lights."

Silence again. Then the woman spoke: "Colonel, our away team brought a copy of the blueprint and the railway doesn't cross our realm at any other point. The actual line is below us and, when that's complete they will abandon these access routes and, in time, we may even be able to use them. Here, let me show you."

There was the twang of bolts being pulled and the door opened outwards. The light was too much and Dan clasped his hands over his face and rolled onto his stomach.

There was no talk now, just movement, and, slowly he turned his head and squinted. The colonel and his two companions had stepped out and were looking down the cul-de-sac to the tunnel.

"Another of their outages," said the woman. "This is storage space coming off the main passage which is, in turn, merely a route from the surface to the tube where the train will connect with Berlin."

She spoke with authority, and the colonel nodded.

"Very good, Frau Huber. But I don't need to remind you of how serious it would be to all of us if you are wrong."

She turned her head away and looked in Daniel's direction and screwed up her face.

"Colonel!" She paused and took a deep breath. "I know my work and I know the tunnels."

"If I may," said the captain, and Frau Huber turned back to the conversation, "we have three people working undercover on the team that is building this railway and they are due here tomorrow for a meeting with the minister. Maybe we could put this on the agenda."

The colonel nodded. "No time to waste!"

Dan held his breath as they went inside, then, quiet as a snake, he crawled into the dark and sat with his knees under his chin.

"Don't close," said the colonel. "Cigarette?"

The trio stepped out again and walked until they reached the edge of the light extending from the doorway. The senior man passed around a pack and struck a match.

Without moving, Daniel peered into the space from whence they had come. Clean as a hospital, the corridor extended as far as he could see, with a high ceiling, polished floor, cream walls shining with enamel, and passages leading off left and right.

There were charts on the walls, but from his oblique line of view, he couldn't make them out. And one framed picture of what seemed to be a man in a brown jacket. Black hair and a shadow on his face. Or was it a moustache? Side-on, he couldn't tell.

As his eyes adjusted, he could see the three more clearly, slim and in dove grey uniforms, with epaulettes and peaked caps for the men while the woman wore a two-piece that showed off her figure.

She dragged her shoe over the soil. "We mustn't

leave any ash," she said as much to herself as to the others.

"Of course," said the colonel, and he and the captain followed her example, then puffed in silence.

"You are new here Frau Huber," said the colonel. "Where were you posted from?"

Frau Huber took the cigarette out of her mouth. "No, I have spent many years in this pod, but I was in charge of data control at the food plant where they process the mushrooms."

"I must salute that wing of the service," said the colonel. "Amazing what they produce. Last night my family and I tried the new pork roast, all from mushrooms and other fungi and you couldn't tell." He took another drag then shifted on his feet. "Mind you, even if I say it, my daughter is an excellent cook."

"Ja, it is amazing," said Frau Huber. "I was not involved with the food itself, but we did get to sample their new ideas. Each year we produce more than 140 million tons of fungi and from it they make every substitute you can imagine."

She moved to the side and leaned against the earth wall, only the slightest hint of light tracing her form.

"You gentlemen both from here?"

"I've been posted all over," said the colonel. "Always in the security wing of excavation, making sure they don't dig us up like termites."

The other two chuckled.

"I'm from Frankfurt," said the captain.

"Children?" asked Frau Huber but, as the captain drew breath, the colonel spoke.

"I have two. My wife would have liked more, but you know the problem. Then she died when one of the tunnels collapsed.

"My eldest, Gretl, is at the Himmler High School and I hope she'll qualify for a scholarship. Her brother shows no such promise, but he makes up for it with sport."

The captain pulled on his cigarette. "I'm sorry colonel. About your wife.

"Me, I'm divorced. My wife stayed under Frankfurt and got married again and she has a son."

"Frankfurt? I envy you," said the woman. "One school trip below Hamburg and that's it. I've spent my whole life under Berlin."

They stood a while, then the colonel waved his hand, the cigarette moving like a laser in the dark.

"This could be dangerous. At last count we had 8,000 kilometres of tunnel, but we've never come so close to rupture."

The captain looked at his watch. "How long do you think we have before they start work down here?"

"Not long enough," said Frau Huber. "Our engineers are coming from all over the Reich to sort it out. They will arrive by morning."

The cigarettes were nearly finished and it wasn't long before the three extinguished the stubs against the wall, and put the remains in their pockets.

"I must return," said the colonel. "Captain, get your engineers to build some sort of camouflage around the door. I would block it up but the Reichs-minister may want to come out here for a look."

"Yes sir," said the captain and he and Frau Huber raised their right arms. "Heil!"

The colonel made the motion as though shooing flies, but said nothing as he vanished down the passage.

The other two waited a moment, then embraced

and kissed for a long time.

"Do you think he suspects?" said the captain.

"I know he doesn't," said Frau Huber. "A friend in security checked his phone taps and there is nothing about us. But he does have a line of women on the side!"

They giggled and the captain pulled her further into the dark.

"You must get on your way," she said without resisting. "You have the documents?"

"Of course, and thank you again? But I must tell you, I am nervous."

"Me too," said Frau Huber. "Oh Dieter," and she pressed into him, "I will miss you, but hopefully it won't be long."

She hugged him and they moved away and stayed out of sight for a minute or more, then returned holding hands and, without looking back, stepped inside. The captain flicked a switch on the wall sending the corridor into darkness though globes remained far down the section, then he closed the door.

In the quiet that followed, Dan lay still and listened to his breathing. The hammers beat softly near the surface and brought a comfort to the dream. Yes, that must be it, characters and a conversation that were nothing more than hops fermenting in his gut and sending their essence to his head.

He stood up slowly and palmed his clothes. The power was still down and the light under the door was gone. Then he remembered his phone. There was no signal underground, but the Nokia had a torch. He pulled it from his pocket and the device came to life with a xylophonic tune.

Daniel turned on the torch and the beam tore through the dark, bouncing against a haze of dust in the air. He was breathing heavily and could hear his pulse. He sucked in and blew out with force as though expelling some demon and the dust danced a jig.

"Okay," he said out loud. "Okay, okay, okay! There is nothing here. There never was and I am alone and I can make it back."

Already he felt better and he took a step and then another, then stopped and turned to where the door had been and shone his torch against the wall.

A faint ridge formed a rectangle, but there were always shapes in the soil. Dogs, cars, faces, he'd seen them all in the wake of a compacter beating the side of a tunnel.

He filled his lungs again then strode purposefully and had almost reached the junction when, with three beeps, the battery died and the dark returned more intense than before.

Daniel dropped his phone and arched backwards like a man shot in the spine. He let out a roar so long that when it finished his head was light with lack of air and, as he breathed in, the anger turned to sobs and down he went, kneeling and folding forward, the bullet now in his gut, and he felt the traffic of tears on his face.

There was nothing in his head and he squeezed his eyelids closed and crossed his arms, hands on shoulders.

He felt the dizziness that comes with crying as it spread through the chest and arms and legs until even his feet were full of air.

Slowly he rolled to a foetal position, shaking and squeezing himself in a hug of misery until he lay still and relaxed.

His lids had been clenched for so long, tiny spots of colour played behind his eyes and now the patterns turned to pastel and then pink, so real he had to look and found the space around him bathed in an aura. So this was death, the beam that draws you into a swirling tube, and he closed his eyes and waited.

"Are you okay?"

The voice was male, spoken in a whisper. Daniel turned his head face down with his arm as a pillow.

"Have you been injured? Do you need a doctor?"

Without moving he tried to speak, but his voice was croaky.

"Very much," he said, then wondered why he had not heard the vehicle coming from the surface.

"Here, I have some water," said the man and he laid his hand on Daniel's shoulder.

"Try to sit up if you can, very slowly."

Daniel squirmed but his muscles were soft and he tried several times before finally rolling onto a hip, eyes still closed.

"Let me turn off the light because it will hurt you," said the man.

Daniel blinked in the dark and felt the steel canteen against his arm. He took it and swigged and the liquid was cool and fresh, but he drank too fast and coughed.

"Good, very good," said the man as he took the bottle.

"Now I am going to turn my torch backwards into the channel behind us so it won't burn too much, then try to open your eyes."

The light went on and Daniel took the slightest glimpse and closed his lids, then opened them again and blinked and wiped his face with the back of his arm.

"That's better! Just breathe easy and see if there is pain anywhere. Can you feel your legs?"

"Yes," said Daniel. "I am not injured."

"Good," said the man. "Would you like some more water?"

He shook his head, and for the first time saw the face of his helper and he screamed and shoveled his feet against the soil, pushing backwards.

He scrambled to a squat, down to a kneel, then up again and ran like a chicken fresh from the chop, bumping into the wall and almost falling. Then turning and trying to regain his balance, but the man was on him, arms around his chest.

The hoarseness remained but Daniel managed a volume that rang in his ears. "Where did you come from?"

He was breathing fast and could taste the water in his throat and it gurgled sour into his mouth and bubbled out as froth around his lips.

"I thought you were a nightmare."

The arm let go and he fell, turning as he landed to roll on his back and he looked up at the captain, now out of uniform and dressed in overalls identical to his own except for the peaked cap with a swastika badge at the front.

The captain knelt beside him.

"Okay, I think maybe you have concussion. Can I just feel your head for bumps?"

"Get off me," said Daniel, but the man continued, running his fingers over the scalp.

"No, nothing there. You say you had a dream?"

Daniel swallowed and half sat up. "I was there, in the passage when you and the colonel and that woman came out."

"Oh, oh well that does rather change things," said the captain. "By law I am now supposed to subdue you by any means, even by death, and take you to my commander."

"Who?" said Daniel. "Who are you? How long have you been down here?"

The man extended his hand and before he knew, Dan was shaking it.

"I am Captain Dieter Bekker."

Silence.

"Sorry, I didn't catch your name," said the captain.

"König. Daniel König." Dan scratched his head and looked again at the overalls. "You are a captain? Is this an army exercise?"

"Oh my goodness," said Dieter. "Of course, I forget, you know nothing of us," and he turned off the torch and sat down.

"Look, I don't know what you and your people are up to," said Daniel, "but I just want to get back to the surface, and I can't without a torch. If you are going that way, can we walk out together?"

"No, rather, let me go back," said Dieter. "This is not the time."

"Back to where. What are you doing down here?"

In the dark it was not possible to see, but there was a shuffling sound as Dieter crawled away and then he flashed the light for a moment. He was sitting with his back against the wall. He patted the soil next to him and Dan moved over.

"Cigarette?"

Daniel ignored him, then felt for the pack and took one. Dieter struck a match and they smoked in silence.

"That feels so good," said Dan.

"Ja, calms the nerves."

It was quiet again, then Dieter spoke.

"This presents a problem. If I let you go and you

report what you saw, you will probably be taken to a psychiatrist, but someone might just come down here for a look, and we need time to seal the entrance."

His tip glowed in the dark and he held the smoke for a long time in his lungs.

"But if my colleagues find me dressed in the overalls of your work team. Ja. Better to be dead!"

Daniel touched Dieter on the shoulder to make sure he really was there.

"You feel real, but you live underground, you want to arrest me and, I think, you are busy running away. Now I know it's a dream."

"For you maybe," said Dieter. "They tell us all the time that we are living the dream in a world built on the sacrifice of those who died to make it so. Sometimes I wish my forebears had perished too."

Daniel spoke slowly. "Now I get it. Of course. These must be the old sewers and the neo-Nazis are meeting down here. I saw the badge on your hat. Just possessing that in Germany, never mind wearing it, could land you in jail."

The captain gurgled like a man being strangled and, unable to contain himself, bellowed down the tunnel, the sound of his mirth bouncing off the walls and scaffolding, off every bucket and wheelbarrow, until it flew back to them like the Valkyries at full tilt with an echo so loud it seemed to shake the earth.

"My dear man, my dear new friend," he said, almost yodeling the words. "It has been so long since I heard such freshness."

Dan wasn't sure whether he was the source of a joke or the butt of it and was glad when Dieter levelled off to a lilting cough and was finally silent.

"Your cigarette has gone out."

"It's okay," said Dan just as the captain struck a match but the flame died.

Dieter leaned forward. "Light off mine," he said and he sucked in.

Their heads came together and, in the glow their eyes met. For all its volume, the laughter had left no glint of joy.

"At the end of the war," said Dieter, then he stopped as though that was the whole tale.

"In 1945, the allies thought Hitler's bunker was the only one, but the Nazis had built a complete system underground. Communication with the surface ended when the country was occupied and some of our soldiers down here didn't even know the war was over.

"They just kept expanding the tunnels and we now have a whole civilization with, I would guess, not more than maybe 300 people left from the old days. We who were born here, well, this is our world."

Dan said nothing.

"I know it sounds amazing to you, but that's the truth."

"That's bullshit," said Daniel. "Where does your electricity come from, your food, uniforms?"

"That's what most people say, and we have had a few who escaped to the surface and told their stories. They are now locked away in asylums. Your asylums.

"Water is plentiful from underground streams, turbines had been built for power as early as the '30s, we have ultraviolet lights for sun and to grow crops and we make our protein from mushrooms. It is a massive operation and not just under Berlin. The network stretches all the way across Germany with high-speed trains between the pods."

"Pods?"

"Ja, that's what they call the towns. We have a big area with flats, schools, shops, and streets, and then a tunnel to the next one."

"And you're still Nazis?"

Dieter grunted. "Nominally. Hitler was mad. If it were not for him, we wouldn't have this divide, you upstairs and us down here. One day I think we'll join, and there have been talks at senior level with your ministers."

"They know?" exclaimed Daniel and he stood up and stretched his legs. "The German government knows about this?"

"Ja, at the top level. They have even paid visits to us, but like yours, our population is in the dark. And they also don't hear about the shopping trips our leaders make outside, their flat-screen TVs tuned to your channels including CNN, holidays to expensive resorts around the world. That's one of the reasons I want to leave, I'm just so sick of hypocrisy."

Daniel knocked his head against the wall, then wished he hadn't because it brought back the pain to his neck. He rolled his shoulders.

"Okay, so tell me how you know all this stuff. There you live, like worms in the ground, everyone blind to what's happening, except, it seems, Dieter Bekker who is even aware of the secret visits by my government."

"That's simple," said Dieter. "For almost ten years, I was aide-de-camp to the general in charge of our army. I got to watch his TV, I kept his diary, I made the appointment when Angela Merkel came to visit.

"Back in 1990, at the time of reunification, I think they hoped the three Germanys could come together. In the end, they decided it was premature and you had your hands full just marrying East and West.

"Also, a lot more of the older generation were still alive and active in our government and you have laws to prosecute Nazis so it would have been difficult. Now most of them are dead and it might be possible."

"Old Nazis?" said Daniel. "The party is growing again you know. In their new form they control much of the far north, some towns. The Hitler salute is banned, but they use it and the police can't arrest everyone."

"I'm sad to hear that," said Dieter. "Maybe they should come to us for a look."

"Oh, it's not hankering for the past so much, just that people are angry and none of the mainstream parties will listen.

"Anyway, tell me about your underworld."

Dieter laughed. "I've never heard it called that.

"Hitler was our founder and we have his picture on all sorts of knick-knacks, even some children's toys, but they took him off the money last year. His birthday is a public holiday but it's moved to the nearest Friday, now called Heritage Weekend.

"The swastika remains on our aluminium flag which is the only way it can fly because there is no wind down here, but they say even that may change. And, when I was a kid, the salute was Heil Hitler. Now it's just Heil. We are prosperous; in recent years we have a lot more freedom within the confines of the state, but it's still a prison because ordinary folk can't visit the surface and most don't even know it's there."

"And the woman?" said Daniel. "The one you were kissing?"

"The lovely Ada Huber. She has access to the machines where they forge German ID documents and even passports for the elite. She made a set for me.

"I leave now and, once I have a life upstairs, she will follow. It is our dream to marry and have a child who is born free."

"But I heard her tell the Colonel she had recently come from your mushroom plant."

"Well what could she say?" said Dieter. "She's actually with our intelligence service and he's under surveillance for holding funds in a US bank account. Streng verboten!"

"How on earth did he set that up?"

"It's not that hard. I have one from when I was with the general."

Dan touched Dieter's cap with his fingers. "We need to make some plans anyway. What to do from here. Have you been 'upstairs' before?"

"Once, when I was at the army staff college in the pod under Leipzig. After our final exam, the top three officer-cadets went on a tour of the city. Very supervised. We saw your world but were not allowed to speak with people or ask questions. Our guide gave us her interpretation: stress, ulcers, debt, children who don't respect their parents, a lack of discipline. All the ills we are not allowed to enjoy."

Daniel kicked the ground. "Not far wrong."

He paused a while, then went on. "Life can be a challenge. I'm divorced but no kids. The break-up was my fault, too much bottle. I have a shit job, my bosses are half my age with a piece of paper to say they're right because they went to college.

"Home for me is a tiny flat in a noisy building full of immigrants who don't or won't speak German and live off my tax bill. My credit card is blown, my health sucks and I'll work all my life then go on a pension that won't feed a cat. Wanna swap?"

"Oh, my friend, you have…"

Daniel cut him off. "I know! They used to complain about that in the DDR. 'In the West, you have a choice.' Today there are people who moan they were better off with the wall and dictatorship and the Stasi because everyone had a job and a house and free medical and a pension.

"Now, all they have is a choice."

"Actually, I was going to say how lucky you are to have a cat."

Daniel shrugged then remembered they were in the dark. "How do you know I have a cat?"

"You said your pension wouldn't be enough to feed it.

"We have cats and dogs, stuffed in museums and my mother said there used to be one or two after the war but they were destroyed by order of the state. No food to waste on pets. My general had some birds in a cage and they used to sing in the office, but at his rank nothing was forbidden. I've read stories of cuddling up with a cat in winter and I did see one when I was in Leipzig, but not close."

Dan felt himself blush. "If I am out late I phone my neighbour, even when I'm drunk, to ask him to feed her. She's called Tina, because that's my favourite singer, Tina Turner. And, yes, she keeps me warm in winter." He chuckled. "You know, that would be my only real worry if you took me prisoner. Who would look after Tina?"

Dieter stood up and brushed his pants. "You're an amazing man, Herr König. If there are people like you on the surface, it makes me want to be there even more."

"I hope you make it," said Daniel. "And you can enjoy the freedom, and the cats."

"It is true," said Dieter. "I do need to be free. You can vote for a better government; we have no elections. You can move to another country; we can't shift to another pod without permission. You can start your own business, but we all work for the state. After the war they wanted people to breed. Now we are only allowed one child unless you are senior like the general, then you get two. I am suffocating!"

"I hope you're not disappointed," said Daniel. "Up there you're still a bird in a cage."

"I'm sure you're right," said Dieter. "But with you, the door is open. You can stay or leave as you wish. We have food and water and a perch to sit on, but birds were made to fly."

Dan felt the air vibrating in his chest. Enough talk. He needed to get out of there. His eyes closed to a squint as the Valkyries beat their wings about his skull and the pain returned.

There was a flicker and the lights came on and both men looked back into the dark of the passage, then the power went off.

Daniel wheezed. His head was on fire.

"They've fixed the problem," and he wiped his eyes. "Electricians are testing the line."

"Well that kills my chance," said Dieter. "I wanted to get out in the dark."

"Where did you get the overalls?"

The captain was silent.

"I saw in the light, they don't fit," he added.

Dieter took a breath and let it out slowly. "We have some of our spies in your workforce. To do that, they need overalls.

"But a favour please. I do want to escape, but I don't want to sell out. I hope you will be discreet."

The hammers were still thudding in the distance and now came the revving of an engine.

"There was a truck of men," said Daniel. "Before the lights went off, they were driving down here to work on the tube. They must have been told the current is about to go on."

"Close your eyes," said Dieter.

Daniel did as he was told and saw a light, pink and pearly through his lids and slowly he opened them just a crack as his pupils adjusted. The lamps were back.

"We have no time," said the captain and he drew another torch from his pocket. "Take this in case they go off again. I must return before I am missed. The colonel has tasked me to camouflage the doorway, so let me do that and maybe I will see you at the surface one day."

"Do you have a pen?"

Dieter produced a pencil and Dan took out his morning rail ticket and wrote his name and number on the back. "If you make it, call me."

The captain threw his arms around Daniel and kissed him on the cheek. "Be safe my friend. I hope to see you soon."

"You too."

Dieter walked up the passage, opened the door and then looked back and waved.

"Heil!" said Daniel and he raised his arm.

Dieter returned the salute. "Freedom!"

The lights flickered but stayed on and their brightness inflamed what was now a migraine.

With another step Dan stumbled and crashed to the ground.

*

The trial was over in minutes. Daniel pleaded guilty, but his state lawyer told the court he had recently lost his job and planned to leave Berlin and make a fresh start somewhere else in Germany after spending a month with his sister in Moscow. And she had agreed to keep his cat until he settled.

"I have listened carefully to your statements and those from counsel," said the judge and she adjusted her glasses.

"We have a rapid rise of neo-Nazis in this country and the movement is more powerful than at any time since the war."

She leaned back in her chair high above the court and took a sip of water.

"People claim no one is listening to their concerns about immigration, unemployment and Germany paying off nations like Greece and Italy. It is hard not to have sympathy with this view.

"There is a cry that mainstream parties ignore these worries, and this is pushing regular people like yourself into the radical wings, left, right, even the Islamic movement. It is only there, in the politics of hate, that anyone hears the angst of the working class.

"I am a lawyer and a judge, I am not a politician, but I do want to say this: our laws banning Nazi propaganda must stay and are not a threat to free speech, but we are seeing a huge increase in these cases, and giving out jail terms will not address the problem." Daniel nodded in agreement.

"It is a matter of record," she continued, "that a rescue team found you semi-comatose in one of the tunnels below the new airport, and a statement from your supervisor backs this up. The medical officer who examined you said you were dehydrated, had five times the legal limit of alcohol in your blood for someone working underground, and had been unconscious for many hours.

"Your squad leader says you wandered away from work. You claim it was because you felt ill and this malady clouded your brain and you were not in control of your actions.

"Nonetheless, repeated absenteeism or being unable to work because of your drinking problem were marked against you, and you were dismissed."

She turned a page in her notes.

"I see you are now under the care of a psychiatrist who is treating your addiction. I have looked over his report and his tests show that you are highly intelligent."

The judge took off her glasses and looked at him. "Yet you choose to work at such a low end of the scale when clearly you could make so much more of your life." She returned to the paper.

"You now attend nightly meetings of Alcoholics Anonymous. I commend you for this and the Court wishes you well. Healing only begins when we admit to having a problem.

"At this stage do you have anything to say, or is any of my information at odds with your recollection?"

Daniel shook his head.

"In that case," and she banged her gavel, "I now give you one month in prison wholly suspended for two years provided you do not reoffend."

Daniel smiled, but the judge fixed him with a stare as she closed the file.

"And please, do not be caught again with this kind of thing on your person."

She held up a clear plastic bag marked Exhibit A. Inside was a small flashlight. Engraved on the handle was a swastika and a likeness of Adolf Hitler.

This is an abridged version. The full story may be published at a later date.

Geoff Hill

Everything Is Ended

The lit match is in my hand
This is my last gasp
Everything is ended
So my words must go too

All my words

My childish dreamings
My teenage fantasies
My adult hopes and fears

My created worlds
My people

They mean nothing

The match falls
The flames rise
Everything is ended

E. E. Blythe

About the Authors

Pam Barton has recently joined the Rugby Cafe Writers' Group and began writing again after many years. She has in the past had a radio programme for children, been a D.J. and put through the landing on the moon for the Australian Radio in the Indian Ocean. On returning to England,  she was a busy parent with John, and became a skin care consultant up to District Manager. After moving again, she went to Luton University for a marketing course. She retired to Rugby with John. Now she is enjoying writing again, painting is also a great pleasure although, as with the writing, hard work is needed.

E. E. Blythe, a poet and member of Rugby Cafe Writers, prefers to write under a pseudonym. Here she explains why: 'Teasing, name-calling, bullying, violence and ridicule necessitated the name for an alias. It was good to stand, impassive, and listen to complimentary comments, and even praise, for poems, songs and stories; and my tormentors had no idea it was me. So when I write, I am E.E.Blythe.'

David J. Boulton took up writing well into retirement from a career in the NHS, so far publishing three historical detective novels. Set in the Peak District, their protagonist has a Quaker background and the books comprise a trilogy. A fourth novel, set in the Second World War, is complete and he has embarked  on a sequel. Alongside General Practice, he and his wife have run a small farm in Northamptonshire for the last thirty years. Of their two grown-up children, one lives in the Peak District with her family, their son completing a five-generation connection for the author with the area.

The Writing Fiction class at the Percival Guildhouse tutored by Gill Vickery has provided the author with encouragement and inspiration, not to mention improving his grammar. *What's all the Fuss About?* has its origins in a class exercise.

Terri Brown - voice actor, artist and author - does not have a book that got her into reading because she doesn't remember a time when she didn't read. Her mother boasts that Terri was reading the likes of Jane Eyre at age seven. First published in a local newspaper aged nine, she caught  the writing bug... she just had some things she needed to do first. A few decades, many adventures and a life

less ordinary later, financed largely by freelance writing, she is ready to start telling her tales with a debut novel, *Shadow Man*, now on sale at Amazon.
www.terri-brown.com

Wendy Goulstone began writing plays from the age of four when given a model theatre, then for performing in story-time in primary school, where she was encouraged by a wonderful headmaster who introduced her to poetry. When eleven years old, she wrote a dramatised version of *Little Women* and a novel about a group of  theatre-mad children. That was a long time ago, but Wendy is a member of Rugby Theatre where she continues to write short plays and organises Open Mics for poets, singers and musicians. Several of her poems have been published in literary magazines and anthologies.

Simon Grenville has lived in Rugby for over twenty years. He has been variously employed as a residential social worker, landscape gardener and Welfare Rights Benefit advisor on disability issues. He has written a number of plays for children including most recently *Searching For The Happiness*, a musical  entertainment drawn from the work of Maurice Maeterlinck which appeared at the Birmingham Children's library, the Midlands Arts

Centre and at St Andrew's Church during the most recent Rugby Festival of Culture.

Originally from Essex, **Christine Hancock** has lived in Rugby for over forty years. A passion for Family History led to an interest in local history, especially that of the town of Rugby. In 2013 she joined a class at the Percival Guildhouse with the aim of writing up her family history research. The class was Writing Fiction and soon she found herself deep in Anglo-Saxon England. Based on the early life of Byrhtnoth, Ealdorman of Essex, who died in 991AD at the Battle of Maldon, the novel grew into a series. She has self-published three volumes and is currently working on the fourth. This short story is based on the prologue, later discarded, of *Bright Sword*, the first of the Byrhtnoth Chronicles.

www.byrhtnoth.com

Born in England, **Desmond Harding** spent his early childhood overseas, giving him the bug for travel. In addition to having worked in the marine industry, acquiring and supplying spares for the larger ships, he has lived in the Middle East, visiting a few countries along the way. There have been a few gentle escapades, boyhood night-time adventures in Kenya, temporarily penniless in Marseille, supervised overnight by armed Iranians on Abu Musa island, and a fire-bomb attempt on the family's Bahrain compound which added to life's rich tapestry. But he must be one of the limited few who have arrived back from the rich Gulf States, landing at Heathrow, destitute and homeless, with a wife and two children barely in their teens. Now retired and living in Rugby with his wife and two cats, replacing the children who have flown the nest, he has self-published two thrillers, available from Amazon, *The Dhow* and *The Irish Prime Minister*. He is now trying to obtain an agent for his third manuscript and is currently working on editing his fourth thriller.

Kate A. Harris and her three siblings lived on their farm until she left home at 16 to follow a career with children. She trained and qualified with Barnardo's, worked as a nursery nurse, and met and married her future Royal Navy husband in Southsea. As a naval wife, she was in Malta with her young family when the  Navy were shutting the naval base. She has two sons and two grandchildren. Kate loves travel including a visit to Sri Lanka when there were hostilities in the country, South Africa, Thailand, and Hong Kong. Kate joined the local newspaper at 50. She enjoyed writing, including property features, Chelsea, and the Gardening Show in Birmingham with Prince Charles and Camilla on the front page. Her Barnardo's two-page spread was published in *The Lady* magazine. Kate attends a Life Writing course where she is enjoying writing features, her family history, memoirs and autobiography.

Cathy Hemsley has been writing short stories and full-length novels for over ten years: inspired by her family history and by her daughter's ideas for a fantasy novel. Two of her stories have been published in *The People's Friend* and she has a book of short stories, *Parable Lives,* published on Amazon. She is preparing a novel  for publication as well as working on a fantasy trilogy. Currently she works as a senior software engineer for GE Power. In addition, she is a member of a local Anglican church and regularly volunteers for a Rugby charity for homeless people.

Geoff Hill is a Zimbabwean writer and journalist living in Johannesburg. He is chief Africa Correspondent for *The Washington Times* (DC) and maintains a second home in Rugby along with a wildlife estate north of Pretoria. In 2000, Geoff became the first non-American to receive a John Steinbeck award for his writing. He has authored two books on Zimbabwe.

John Howes is a former local
newspaper journalist and website
editor now working as a teacher. He
has self-published two books - *We
Believe*, a collection of his writings on
spirituality, and a guide on how to
teach poetry. He runs a poetry
website for teachers, a blog of
reflections on Christianity and a
collection of stories for children about the Holocaust.
He plays the piano and writes music for schools and
choirs. John is working on a spiritual memoir and a
book about the Gospel of St Luke. This is one of his first
attempts in the short story genre.

oadonai.wordpress.com

Ruth Hughes was born in 1946. She was a bulge baby
which is lucky as she is 5ft and rather roundish. From
about seven, she wanted to milk cows and worked on
farms around Warwickshire. She married a farmworker,
and has lived with her husband Monty in their tied
house for 53 years now. They have three children, five
grandchildren and one new great-grandchild. She loves
her village, her family and writing.

Theresa Le Flem, a novelist, artist and
poet, always wanted to be a writer. She
lives in the Midlands, in the UK, with
her husband Graham, an electrical
engineer. With four novels now
published, and also an anthology of her
poetry and drawings, her dream was
first fulfilled when her first novel was

accepted and published by Robert Hale Ltd. She never looked back. Born in London into an artistic family, daughter of the late artist Cyril Hamersma, she has three children and five grandchildren all who live abroad in America and New Zealand. Her creative life began by writing poetry, painting and later in running her own studio pottery in Cornwall. But she has had a succession of jobs too – from factory-work, antiques, retail sales, veterinary receptionist and sewing machinist to hairdressing. Over three years ago, Theresa formed a group of local writers, Rugby Café Writers, who meet fortnightly to talk about their work over a coffee. Writing remains her true passion.

Married to a Guernsey man, Theresa shares a love of the sea with her husband and recently they have bought an almost derelict cottage in Guernsey. Gradually they are working to bring it back to life. Situated only a short walk to the sea, it might one day become the perfect writer's retreat where a new novel might emerge out of the dust and cobwebs.

Theresa is a member of the Romantic Novelists' Association, the Society of Authors and The Poetry Society.

https://theresaleflem.wordpress.com

Madalyn Morgan was brought up in a pub in the market town of Lutterworth. Her dream was to be an actress. Her mother wanted her to have a 'proper' job so she became a hairdresser. Eight years later, aged twenty-four, she gave up a successful salon and wig-hire business for a place at Drama College and a career

as an actress. In 2010, after living in London for thirty-six years, she moved back to Lutterworth. She is currently writing her eighth novel, as well as a memoir of short stories, articles, poems, photographs and character breakdowns, written when she was acting.

madalynmorgan.wordpress.com

Fran Neatherway grew up in a small village in the middle of Sussex. She studied History at the University of York and put her degree to good use by working in IT. Reading is an obsession – she reads six or seven books a week. Her favourites are crime, fantasy and science fiction. Fran has been writing for thirty-odd  years, short stories at first. She has attended several writing classes and has a certificate in Creative Writing from Warwick University. She has completed three children's novels, as yet unpublished, and is working on the first draft of an adult novel. Fran has red hair and lives in Rugby with her husband and no cats.

Bella Osborne has been jotting down stories as far back as she can remember but decided that 2013 would be the year she finished a full-length novel. Since then, she's written five best-selling romantic comedies and been shortlisted three times for the RNA Contemporary Romantic Novel of the Year Award.  Bella's stories are about friendship, love and coping with what life throws at you. She lives in the Midlands,

UK with her husband, daughter and a cat who thinks she's a dog. When not writing, Bella is usually eating biscuits and planning holidays.

www.bellaosborne.com

Born in Bedfordshire to a French mother and English father, **Sandrine Pickering** enjoyed a very varied childhood in Yorkshire, Rutland and Warwickshire, with school holidays in France. Upon leaving Rugby High School, she read Biological Sciences at both the University of East Anglia (UEA) and Aix-Marseilles as an Erasmus exchange student, and  completed her teacher training at Cambridge University. She has worked in marketing, PR, educational publishing, event management, teaching and complementary therapies. She has always enjoyed writing, and now, as the mother of eight-year-old twins, she is exploring memoire and children's story writing.

Lindsay Woodward has had a lifelong passion for writing, starting off as a child when she used to write stories about the Fraggles of *Fraggle Rock*. Knowing there was nothing else she'd rather study, she did her degree in writing and has now turned her favourite hobby into a career. She writes from her home in Rugby, where she lives with her husband and cat. Her debut novel,  *Bird*, was published in April 2016 and Lindsay is now working on her seventh novel. Her short story, *Bird,* is the original inspiration for the novel.

Chris Wright was born in the wagon of a travelling show and raised on Brummies' tales of Welsh gypsies, lead zeppelins, dangling cables that shredded the factories of the first world war and great grandfathers lost coming home to find their wives remarried and doing very nicely thank you! He stopped wanting to be  a shepherd when an escaped flock stopped the Tesco man from delivering his olives. Never mind Mr two-brains, Chris has seven brains: jester, logical, musical, word-brain, bread-head, portable idiot, says his wife and a membrane to contain the conflict. Likes include Love, the Sea, Fishes, Wishes, Jokes, mellow folks, olives, originals, Aboriginals, fun and Brum.

Printed in Great Britain
by Amazon